THE ORGANS OF CAMBRIDGE

The Organs of Cambridge

An Illustrated Guide to the Organs of the University and City of Cambridge

Nicholas Thistlethwaite

Series Editor: John Brennan

POSITIF PRESS · OXFORD

To

B. B. EDMONDS

(1910–2003)

with affection and gratitude

Front cover: The organ in King's College Chapel.
(Photograph by John Brennan)

Back cover: The organ in the church of St Mary the Less,
casework designed by Lawrence Bond (1978) containing a new organ
built by Kenneth Tickell & Company Ltd in 2006–7.
(Photograph supplied by Kenneth Tickell)

Frontispiece: A photograph (*c.*1900) showing the interior of
King's College Chapel, looking west. *(Positif Press)*

Positif Press · 130 Southfield Road · Oxford · OX4 1PA · England

ISBN 978 0 906894 39 2

Designed and produced by John Brennan at the Positif Press, Oxford.
Typeset in Trump Mediæval
Printed and bound by Biddles Limited, King's Lynn

CONTENTS

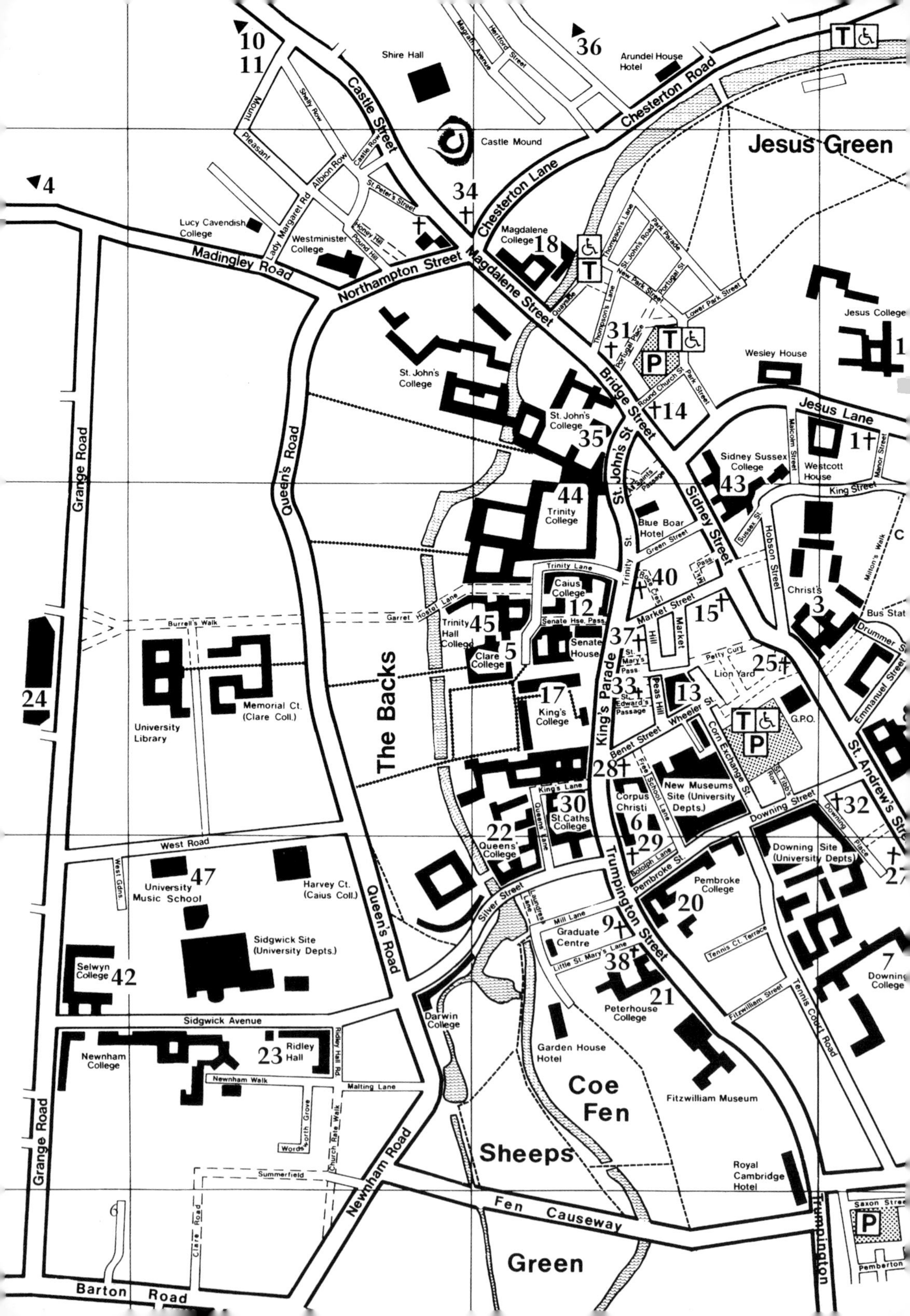

10
11
36
4
Shire Hall
Arundel House Hotel
Castle Street
Castle Mound
Chesterton Road
Chesterton Lane
Jesus Green
Mount Pleasant
Shelly Row
Albion Row
Castle Row
St. Peter's Street
Lady Margaret Rd
Honey Hill
Pound Hill
Lucy Cavendish College
Westminister College
Madingley Road
Northampton Street
Magdalene Street
Magdalene College
18
34
Thompson's Lane
St. John's Road
Park Parade
New Park Street
Portugal St.
Lower Park Street
Quayside
31
Portugal Place
Round Church St.
Park Street
Jesus College
Wesley House
St. John's College
Bridge Street
14
Jesus Lane
Malcolm Street
Manor Street
1
Westcott House
Sidney Sussex College
43
King Street
St. John's College
35
44
Trinity College
St. John's St
All Saints Passage
Blue Boar Hotel
Green Street
Sidney Street
Sussex St.
Hobson Street
Milton's Walk
Christ's
3
Bus Stat
Drummer St
Trinity Lane
Trinity St.
Rose Cres.
40
Hill Pass.
Caius College
12
Market Street
15
Market Hill
Garret Hostel Lane
Burrell's Walk
Trinity Hall College
45
Senate Hse. Pass.
Senate House
37
St. Mary's Pass.
Petty Cury
Lion Yard
25
Emmanuel Street
Clare College
5
King's Parade
33
St. Edward's Passage
Peas Hill
13
Wheeler St.
G.P.O.
The Backs
17
King's College
Corn Exchange St.
Benet Street
St. Tibbs Row
24
Memorial Ct. (Clare Coll.)
University Library
Queen's Road
Grange Road
28
Free School Lane
New Museums Site (University Depts.)
St. Andrew's Street
32
King's Lane
30
St. Caths College
Queens' Lane
Corpus Christi
6
29
Downing Street
Downing Place
22
Queens' College
Botolph Lane
Pembroke St.
Downing Site (University Depts)
27
West Road
West Gdns.
47
University Music School
Harvey Ct. (Caius Coll.)
Silver Street
Laundress Lane
Trumpington Street
Pembroke College
20
Mill Lane
9
Graduate Centre
Little St. Mary's Lane
38
Tennis Ct. Terrace
7
Downing College
Sidgwick Site (University Depts.)
Selwyn College
42
Darwin College
21
Peterhouse College
Sidgwick Avenue
Fitzwilliam Street
Tennis Court Road
Newnham College
Ridley Hall Rd
23
Ridley Hall
Garden House Hotel
Newnham Walk
Malting Lane
Coe Fen
Fitzwilliam Museum
Wordsworth Grove
Church Rate Walk
Sheeps
Royal Cambridge Hotel
Summerfield
Newnham Road
6
Clare Road
Fen Causeway
Trumpington
Saxon Street
Pemberton
Green
Barton Road
Road

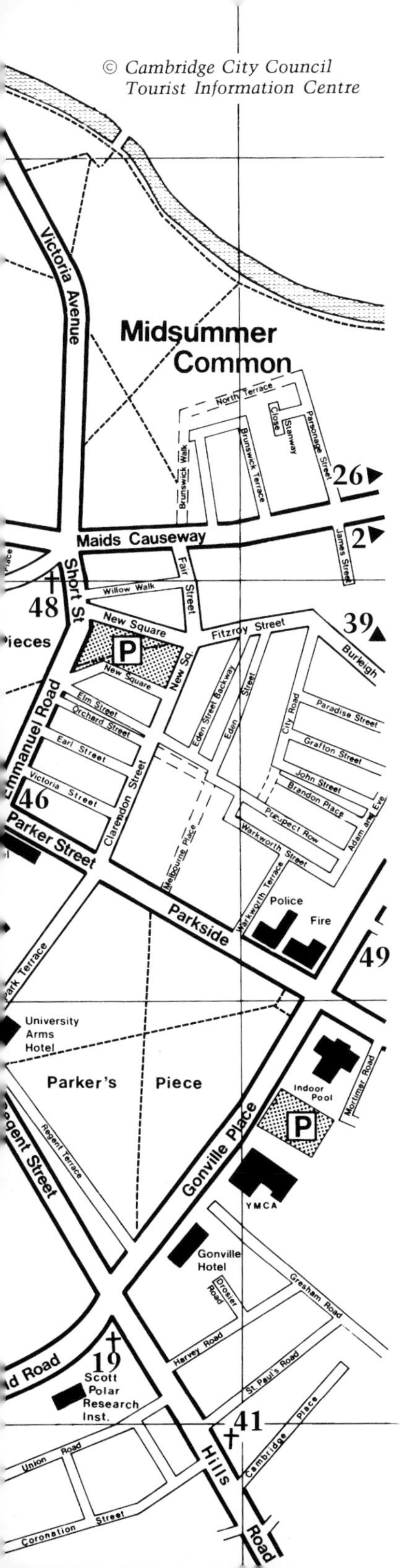

CAMBRIDGE ORGANS

Map Key

1 All Saints' Church
2 Christ Church
3 Christ's College Chapel
4 Churchill College Chapel
5 Clare College Chapel
6 Corpus Christi College Chapel
7 Downing College Chapel
8 Emmanuel College Chapel
9 Emmanuel United Reformed Church
10 Fitzwilliam College Chapel
11 Girton College Chapel
12 Gonville and Caius College Chapel
13 The Guildhall
14 Holy Sepulchre Church
15 Holy Trinity Church
16 Jesus College Chapel
17 King's College Chapel
18 Magdalene College Chapel
19 The Church of Our Lady and the English Martyrs
20 Pembroke College Chapel
21 Peterhouse Chapel
22 Queens' College Chapel
23 Ridley Hall Chapel
24 Robinson College Chapel
25 St Andrew the Great
26 St Andrew the Less
27 St Andrew's Street Baptist Church
28 St Bene't's Church
29 St Botolph's Church
30 St Catharine's College Chapel
31 St Clement's Church
32 St Columba's United Reformed Church
33 St Edward's Church
34 St Giles' Church
35 St John's College Chapel
36 St Luke's Church
37 St Mary the Great
38 St Mary the Less
39 St Matthew's Church
40 St Michael's Church
41 St Paul's Church
42 Selwyn College Chapel
43 Sidney Sussex College Chapel
44 Trinity College Chapel
45 Trinity Hall Chapel
46 Unitarian Church
47 University Music School
48 Wesley Church
49 Zion Baptist Church

PREFACE

THE first edition of this book appeared in 1983. Twenty-five years have elapsed since then. Nine of the organs it described have been replaced, and others have received additions or undergone renovation. Research has also advanced. More is now known about the music (and organs) of the college chapels in the early seventeenth century as a result of the work of Dr Ian Payne, and the new edition of William Dowsing's journal of destruction, edited by Trevor Cooper, has cast further light on a murky subject. Both writers have drawn attention to the importance of Harleian MS 7019 ('Innovations in Religion & abuses in Government in ye University of Cambridge') and a number of useful college histories have appeared. I myself have been able to explore certain college archives in greater depth, and this has yielded interesting material, not all of which, however, can be fully accommodated here.

For all these reasons, the time is ripe for a new edition. The format remains unchanged, but all the entries have been revised or replaced, and the information recorded is as up to date as I can make it. Yet even as we go to press, there are rumours of two new organs ...

Neither this book nor its predecessor could have been written without the co-operation and assistance of many people. I have acknowledged the help which particular individuals have given me at the end of the text, and I take this opportunity of thanking all those organ-builders, clergy, organists and organ scholars who kindly replied to my enquiries or gave me access to instruments in their care. My principal debt is acknowledged in the dedication of this book to someone whose generosity in placing his encyclopaedic knowledge of English organs at the disposal of others was well known. I should like also to thank Michael Sayer and David Wickens for their patient work in transcribing material from the British Organ Archive at various times. José Hopkins and the late Stephen Bicknell each made valuable suggestions and supplied information for this second edition, and the archivists I have encountered have been invariably helpful. Finally, I am grateful to John Brennan for undertaking a new edition of this book, and for the care with which he has prepared the manuscript for publication (to say nothing of taking some of the photographs himself).

There are many organs in Cambridge, not all of them of great interest. My policy has been to include details of all the organs in the colleges of the University, and all those in the ancient parish churches of the town of Cambridge. Otherwise, I have selected instruments which seem to me to be of some interest.

This book, like its predecessor, will inevitably include errors and omissions: I hope they will be of only minor significance, but it goes without saying that I will be grateful to be told of them.

Nicholas Thistlethwaite

INTRODUCTION

THIS brief survey is intended to establish the context of the historical material and specifications which follow. In some respects, Cambridge presents a microcosm of organ-building in England over the last five centuries, and, as such, it lends detail to the broader picture. In other respects, Cambridge organ-building has proved idiosyncratic, something to be understood only with reference to the particular circumstances of an ancient university and East Anglian market town. This introduction therefore attempts both to underline developments common to English organ-building as a whole, and also to point out features peculiar to Cambridge. It is hoped that the book will thereby prove more generally useful than a simple collection of stop lists and photographs.

We know little of real significance about organs and organ-building in Cambridge before 1660. Physical evidence is almot totally lacking. Earlier claims that three extant cases pre-date 1640 now seem problematic. The King's main case may incorporate elements of Thomas Dallam's work (1605–6) but in its present form it probably dates from the 1680s. The Framlingham case (formerly in Pembroke College) is most likely Thamer's work of *c.*1675. Only the former St John's College case (now at Old Bilton) perhaps survives from the 1630s, although a post-Restoration date cannot be altogether ruled out. The question acquires additional importance from the fact that Robert Dallam's stop list of 1635–6 is recorded. It is the only piece of substantial evidence that we have for the kind of organ which was familiar to Cambridge organists (the Tomkins and Loosemore families, for instance) in the early seventeenth century. The accounts for Dallam's instrument at King's tell us much about the building of the organ, but virtually nothing about the organ itself.

All other documentary evidence is scanty and deals largely with organs which were permanent fixtures in a parish church or college chapel. It confirms the generally-accepted picture of the consequences of the Reformation for organ-building in England: organs were being built and maintained into the 1540s; following uncertainty during the middle years of the century, the Elizabethan Settlement consolidated the Protestant victory, and organs – reinstated during the reign of Queen Mary – began to fall into disuse (Great St Mary's, by 1583) or were disposed of under the influence of radical reformers (King's 1570). In Cambridge, the reinvigoration of the musical foundation at Trinity College under the influence of Dr Thomas Nevile (appointed Master in 1593) proved to be a watershed, and organs gradually found their way back into the college chapels as a more liturgical style of worship was adopted. The trickle became a flood in the 1630s, when six colleges acquired new organs, only to be abruptly halted in the early 1640s as the Parliamentarians and their allies gained the upper hand and the notorious William Dowsing was sent to purge the college chapels of popish excesses. He found most of the organs gone. Yet this is to say nothing about the use of organs in a secular context.

Even when the influence of Puritanism was at its height in the 1640s and 50s organs survived for domestic music-making. The use of an organ in the chapel may have been discontinued, but an organ may have survived in the Master's Parlour or the Combination Room.

A further misunderstanding needs to be dispelled. The chapel organs were not necessarily destroyed when they were prudently dismantled in the early 1640s. Eight colleges seem to have had organs in 1640, and of these five probably reinstated the old organ (wholly or in part) at the Restoration. Only in one instance is it known for certain that the former organ was not replaced. This was Peterhouse, where the Fellows decided during the 1650s to sell the chapel organ which had been taken down and stored in the Library.

The use of organs in worship became acceptable again after 1660, and in Cambridge the chief beneficiaries were two local organ-builders – Thomas Thamer (first heard of in Cambridge when he did work at Christ's in 1658) and Lancelot Pease, who had taken the old Peterhouse organ down to London sometime before 1660. Pease built a new Chair Organ at King's in 1661, and may have done other work reinstating and repairing organs, but by the mid-1660s he seems to have taken up residence in Dublin, leaving the field clear for Thamer. From the slight evidence that has survived, we may guess that Thamer's work was conservative and of no great technical sophistication; the one surviving specification of a Thamer organ (Winchester Cathedral, 1665–70) shows little advance, beyond the inclusion of a single mixture, on the organs being built before the Rebellion. Yet for a quarter of a century, Thamer must have satisfied the college organists, because until his death at Ely in 1685 none of the London builders is known to have undertaken significant work in Cambridge. His name appears alongside payments for tuning or repairs at Christ's, St John's, Queens' and Jesus; he built a new Chair Organ at Trinity in 1662–3, a new Great Organ (?) at King's during the mid-1670s, and new organs at Peterhouse (1667) and Pembroke (1675). Unattributed organs at Corpus (1662) and Magdalene (1677) may have been his work, and it has been suggested that he built a Chair Organ at St John's College.

It may be a measure of Thamer's competence that within ten years of his work at King's, Renatus Harris was called in to undertake a major reconstruction of the instrument; the specification is lost, but, as with the organ built by Harris' rival, Bernard ('Father') Smith, for Trinity College in 1706–8, both in size and in composition, this instrument must have represented a significant departure from the conservative tradition which had become entrenched in Cambridge through Thamer's influence. By the 1680s organists were looking for more variety of tone and greater flexibility than the earlier tradition could offer, and they would find both in the mixtures, mutations and reeds of the organs made by Smith and Harris. The organs of King's, Great St Mary's and Trinity demonstrated this new style, imported from London. Other Cambridge organs, built during the years following Thamer's death, showed a less marked London influence, not least in the casework, which has a slightly old-fashioned, provincial feel about it. This, and confusing documentary evidence, makes for uncertainty concerning the original builders of a number of organs whose cases survive today at Emmanuel, Christ's and Pembroke College. Charles Quarles, Organist of Trinity College (1688–1717), was named as supplier of the two latter instruments, and he appears in the records of other colleges receiving payments for maintaining organs, but his precise status is obscure. Whatever the truth, it is clear that by the early eighteenth century, Cambridge had both old and new style instruments, London work and provincial work.

In organ-building activity, as in other areas, the eighteenth century was a period of decline for Cambridge. Henry Turner (originally Heinrich Tolner, a German immigrant) and his son Barnard maintained and repaired organs in and around the town until Barnard's death in 1776, when they were succeeded by the Humphrey Argents, father and son. Queens' (1710) and Peterhouse (1765) acquired new organs, but in other colleges organs were disposed of (Corpus Christi, Jesus) or fell into disuse (Pembroke, and, a little later, Emmanuel and Christ's). William Cole commented that the singing of metrical psalms fell out of favour within the University in the mid-eighteenth century, and so there was little use for an organ in those chapels which did not maintain the choral service.

Attention now switches from the colleges to the parish churches. Most had been without an organ since the second half of the sixteenth century, but during the early years of the nineteenth century nearly all the Cambridge churches acquired either a barrel or finger organ; by 1840, only two of the ancient parish churches were without one. Great St Mary's had had the use of the University Organ since 1698 and paid an organist to accompany the parish services. Three other churches seem to have had organs before the end of the eighteenth century: All Saints', St Michael's, and Holy Trinity. St Andrew the Great followed in 1810, and then the remainder of the churches during the 1820s and 30s – St Bene't (1827), St Mary the Less (*c.*1830), St Botolph (1833), St Edward (1838) and Holy Sepulchre (by 1840). Most of these instruments stood in a gallery at the west end of the church; none of them had more than one manual-and-a-half of keys and rudimentary 'pull-down' pedals. Modest in scale, they were modest in another sense as well. An unidentified writer of 1839 made no bones about their shortcomings, and referred scathingly to the cause:

> It is sad to see now-a-days Music as well as Architecture injured by the system of contracts; we allude just now to organ-builders, who, instead of being induced to furnish good instruments by a prospect of a fair recompense, are led to take advantage of the almost complete ignorance generally existing in parishes, to furnish only as much as they can afford without being absolute losers by the agreement.[1]

His complaint referred to the convention whereby churchwardens sought tenders for an organ, it being understood by both parishioners and the competing organ-builders that the lowest tender would, as a matter of course, be accepted. By such an iniquitous system, commented this writer, the builder of the St Botolph's organ lost money on the contract, and had the builder of the otherwise 'very good' organ in St Michael's not been obliged to reduce his estimate, 'the reed work would have been quite, instead of nearly finished'. But not everyone was so demanding. Commenting on Lincoln's little organ in Holy Trinity, the writer remarked, 'Of this instrument ... nothing need be said, but that, whether it be in tune or not, whether in repair or needing it, the congregation seem equally unconscious and indifferent'.

Within the University, indifference towards the use of organs in worship was passing by the middle of the nineteenth century. The colleges with choral foundations had kept their chapel organs in repair, and King's had spent over £850 on a new instrument in 1802–5, but from the mid-1840s onwards a number of colleges which had either never had an organ or had dispensed with one, acquired a new instrument (Jesus 1849, Corpus Christi 1855, St Catharine's 1863, Gonville & Caius 1865, Clare 1874) and others saw the restoration of an organ which had fallen into disuse (Christ's and Pembroke 1865, Emmanuel 1871). The explanation is not far to seek. University life was reviving under the impact of reforms which reversed one hundred and fifty years of decline, and within the Church of England there was a new concern for decency and order in worship, bringing with it a new awareness of the contribution which choral and congregational music could make.

Money seems not to have been a problem. In the course of just over a century (1801–1913) the Trinity College organ was in the hands of organ-builders on no fewer than thirteen occasions; of these, six involved major reconstruction with extensive tonal alterations, and complete or partial replacement of the action. The organ-builder most closely associated with the Trinity organ during this period was William Hill (1789–1870). He and his son Thomas (1822–93) exercised a considerable influence on organ-building in Cambridge throughout the Victorian era – between 1840 and 1890 nearly all the important work within the University was undertaken by their firm. Initially, the Hills' influence was progressive, even radical. Thus, at William Hill's hands, the compasses of Cambridge organs were reduced from the old English GG, FF or CC to a uniform C-compass, the Swell Organs were made full-compass and given a complete flue chorus in imitation of the Great, and an independent Pedal Organ with a 'German' pedal board was provided (e.g. King's, 1859). In other respects, though, both Hills were conservatives, something which becomes obvious when their work is compared with that of a younger contemporary such as Henry Willis (1821–1901). They restored the old organs at Christ's, Pembroke and Emmanuel, and reconstructed the Smith organ in Great St Mary's, retaining as much old pipework as possible and matching new work to the old. Even in their more 'modern' rebuilds (Trinity and St John's) they demonstrated an attachment to properly-developed flue choruses, low wind-pressures, and restraint in the provision of console accessories.

This approach found little favour with the generation of organists which came to prominence in Cambridge round about 1890. The new fashion was for large organs with pneumatic actions, plenty of accessories to facilitate frequent changes of registration, extensive enclosure, and tonal schemes which offered every effect from a massive tutti to ethereal accompanimental strings. Under the influence of Dr A. H. Mann (King's), Dr Alan Gray (Trinity), Dr Cyril Rootham (St John's) and E. W. Naylor (Emmanuel) old organs were rebuilt and new organs commissioned in conformity with this new taste. During the 1890s and early 1900s much of the work fell to Norman & Beard of Norwich: the powerful yet bright tone of their instruments, together with their mechanical innovations and sophisticated consoles, were approved of, and they built eight new, or largely new organs for the colleges in the course of twenty years. However, a new influence began to make itself felt with the completion of Harrison & Harrison's rebuilding of the Ely Cathedral organ in 1907. Following a small new organ for Girton in 1909, Harrison rebuilt the Clare organ (1911), and then in 1913 the firm reconstructed the Trinity College organ to a typical Arthur Harrison scheme. Other major work followed after the 1914–18 war, culminating in the complete rebuilding of the old Hill organ in King's in 1934. Although a little altered subsequently, it survives today as a worthy monument to an important (though now largely obscured) era in Cambridge's organ-building history.

The second half of the twentieth century witnessed unprecedented organ-building activity in Cambridge. The large romantic organs of the Edwardian and inter-war years were dismantled to be replaced, first, by even larger eclectic instruments with non-mechanical actions, and then by mechanical action organs with (sometimes) more disciplined specifications. All but two of the college chapels (King's and Queens') have seen the installation of a new organ or the extensive reconstruction of an existing one, and several have experienced both.

The rebuilding of the St John's College organ (1955) initiated the first phase. With its solo mutations, neo-classical mixtures, and a sprinkling of Germanic nomenclature, it introduced a generation of Cambridge organ students to the principles which had governed the design of the Royal Festival Hall organ, opened the previous year. Other rebuilds in a similar style followed: Corpus Christi (1959), Emmanuel College (1963), St Edward's Church (1964), and then, in 1968, a completely new organ for Corpus – a lavish design, with an eclectic specification, a Choir Organ in the traditional *rückpositiv* position behind the player, and a console amply provided with playing aids. The second phase was inaugurated with the opening of the new organ in Clare College in March 1971. This instrument incorporated two features which were to become characteristic of the organs built in Cambridge during the next few decades, and, further, it suggested a significant development. The two features were mechanical key action and the total encasement of the organ. The development was the willingness of Cambridge musicians to look outside the British Isles when choosing an organ-builder, with the result that eight colleges have now commissioned organs from abroad: Germany (Clare and Caius), Switzerland (Trinity, Girton and Jesus), Denmark (Robinson and Trinity Hall) and Canada (Selwyn).

One other development should be noted. In several instances the survival of earlier material has prompted a desire to work in a particular historical style. To an extent this was the case at Trinity (though some of the Smith registers have been transposed down an octave) but the approach was adopted most consistently at Pembroke and Magdalene, where new pipework was made to scales used by Bernard Smith in the seventeenth century. Less rigorous essays in historical reconstruction are to be found at Christ's and Emmanuel College, though in both places surviving seventeenth-century cases have been handsomely restored to their original proportions and appearance.

Other new organs have adopted a contemporary aesthetic. This includes all the imported instruments, with the exception of the Metzler in Trinity, and also organs by Kenneth Jones, Kenneth Tickell and Peter Collins in (respectively) Great St Mary's, Little St Mary's and Fitzwilliam College. The latter is particularly interesting as a collaboration between a renowned modern architectural practice and an innovative organ-builder. By contrast, the (largely new) organ for St John's College was designed and voiced in the style of Hill because that was felt to be appropriate to the instrument's principal musical function – the accompaniment of the college's world-famous choir.

Restoration has also featured in recent years. The term is used with varying degrees of precision but includes work on the Willis organ in Emmanuel URC, the University Organ in Great St Mary's, the Binns in Queens' and the Abbott & Smith instrument in Our Lady and the English Martyrs.

The result of all this activity is that Cambridge today offers an illuminating snapshot of the recent history of organ-building in England and further afield. Unsurprisingly, there have been both successes and failures. A number of influences have affected the course of events – a growing interest in historical performance practice, ease of travel abroad for both student and teacher, regular visits by distinguished recitalists and tutors – but also the persistent influence of Anglican choral music and the aspiration of many organ scholars to make a career in the cathedral organ loft. As a consequence of these diverse influences, there is today a greater variety of organs in Cambridge than ever before.

'I am much pleased with the Organs here', wrote Samuel Wesley to his friend Vincent Novello whilst on a visit to Cambridge in the summer of 1825. Perhaps no one would feel able to offer so unqualified a judgement today, but there is still much among the Cambridge organs to give pleasure and to provide interest to performer, listener and critic.

SOURCES AND ABBREVIATIONS

This new edition of *The Organs of Cambridge* includes documentary sources for many of the instruments described. These lists are not definitive, but are intended to provide a starting-point for more detailed study. The following abbreviations are employed:

- BL British Library (St Pancras, London)
- BOA British Organ Archive (Birmingham Central Library)
- CCRO Cambridge County Record Office (Shire Hall, Cambridge)
- CGA *Cambridge General Advertiser*
- CUL Cambridge University Library
- JWD Trevor Cooper (editor), *The Journal of William Dowsing* (Woodbridge 2001)
- O&A Nicholas Thistlethwaite, 'Organs and Arminians in seventeenth-century Cambridge', in John Ogasapian *et al* (eds), *Litterae Organi: Essays in honor of Barbara Owen* (OHS Press, Richmond, Virginia 2005)
- RCM Royal College of Music
- RCO Royal College of Organists
- W&C Robert Willis & John Willis Clark, *The Architectural History of the University of Cambridge*, 3 vols (Cambridge 1886)

A select bibliography will be found on page 151.

LIST OF ORGANS

Trinity College Chapel (c.1865), the organ before it was rebuilt by Hill in 1870.

ALL SAINTS' CHURCH — Jesus Lane

The organ was built by Forster & Andrews for Bodley's new church in 1864. In the early years of the twentieth century A.T. Miller & Son removed the organ to its present location on the south side of the chancel, added the Pedal Bourdon, and gave the Swell an independent bottom octave by completing three of the registers. An unexecuted design for an oak organ screen by Bodley (1905) is probably contemporary with this work. The church was declared redundant in 1973 and is now vested in the Churches Conservation Trust.

GREAT	
Open Diapason	8
Stopped Diapason	8
Dulciana (grooved)	8
Principal	4
Harmonic Flute	4
Twelfth	2²/3
Fifteenth	2
Mixture	III
Trumpet	8
Spare (formerly Krumhorn)	

SWELL	
Double Diapason (c)	16
Open Diapason (c)	8
Stopped Diapason	8
Principal	4
Mixture	III
Cornopean (c)	8
Oboe (c)	8

PEDAL	
Open Diapason	16
Bourdon	16

COUPLERS
Swell to Great
Great to Pedal
Swell to Pedal

ACTION
Tracker

COMPASS
Manuals: C–g^3
Pedal: C–f^1

ACCESSORIES
Three combination pedals to Great

Left and right:
Two views of the organ in Little Bardfield Church, Essex. In 1790 this instrument was presented to All Saints' Church, Cambridge by Jesus College. It was removed to Little Bardfield in 1865.

Previous organs

The old All Saints' Church stood in Trinity Street, opposite Trinity College. In 1685 the Vestry agreed to raise a voluntary subscription for an organ, and awarded an allowance of twenty-four shillings a quarter to Alexander Norfolk, the 'player'. Nothing further is known of this instrument, though there is a reference in 1774 to an organ loft. In 1790, Jesus College made 'a present of the remains of our Organ to the Parish of All Saints in Cambridge'. The gift was accepted and the instrument was put into some sort of repair until in 1830 John Gray was paid £140 for 'a new inside'. When the old church was pulled down in 1865 the organ was sold to the parish of Little Bardfield, Essex, where it still stands.

CCRO: All Saints, Cambridge – Minute Books, 1611–1832, 1832–65
Jesus College Archives: Conclusion Book (1790)
BOA: Gray & Davison – Ledger 1: 92

CHRIST CHURCH — Newmarket Road

The organ was built by William Hill in 1839. In 1980 Norman Hall & Sons electrified the pedal action, and at the same time removed the larger Open Diapason from the Great to provide an extension rank in the Pedal.

GREAT		
No. 2 Open Diapason [*sic*]	8	
Stop Diapason bass / Stop Diapason treble	8	
Dulciana	8	
Principal	4	
Wald Flute	4	
Twelfth	$2^2/_3$	
Fifteenth	2	

PEDAL		
Open Diapason (wood)	16	
Bourdon	16	A
Principal	8	B
Bass Flute	8	A
Fifteenth	4	B
Choral Bass	4	A

COUPLERS

Swell to Great
Great to Pedal
Swell to Pedal
Swell Octave

SWELL	
Double Diapason	16
Open Diapason (c)	8
Stop Diapason bass / Stop Diapason treble	8
Orchestral Gamba	8
Voix Celeste (c)	8
Principal	4
Mixture	II
Horn	8
Oboe	8
Clarion	4

COMPASS

Manuals: C–f^3
Pedal: C–f^1

ACTION

Manuals and stops: tracker
Pedal: electric

ACCESSORIES

Three combination pedals to each manual
One reversible pedal: Great to Pedal

History

Professor Walmisley secured William Hill the contract to build an organ for the new church in the suburb of Barnwell in 1839. It had a GG-compass Great, a tenor-c Swell with four stops, and an octave-and-a-half of Pedal Pipes (the lowest of which were unisons). Buckingham added a Trumpet in place of a Dulciana in 1844 under the supervision of R.H. Wood of St John's College. Two years later (1846) Gray & Davison supplied Wood with the pipework and components of a 12-stop Swell; it had been substituted for Hill's by the time Sperling recorded the stop list *c.*1850. Despite subsequent rebuilds by Miller (1880), Bedwell (1898), and again Miller (1932) much of Hill's work, including the central section of the case, survives.

The building was sub-divided in 1973. The church (with the organ still in the original west gallery) occupies the upper floor.

BOA: Hill, Norman & Beard archive – Hill Letter Book (1838–61): 66
BOA: Gray & Davison archive – Shop Book 2: 63; Ledger 4: 243
BL: Sperling Notebooks, vol. 2: 34.
L.S. Barnard, 'Buckingham's Travels – Part IX', in *The Organ*, vol. 54 (1975): 46

Left: The Hill organ in Christ Church

CHRIST'S COLLEGE CHAPEL — St Andrew's Street

The organ was built in 1983 by Bishop & Son of Ipswich. It incorporates four registers (*) from the organ of 1705, and four others (†) of eighteenth century origin. The case also survives and has been restored to its original proportions.

GREAT	
Open Diapason	8 *
Stopped Diapason	8 †
Principal	4 *
Flute	4 †
Twelfth	$2^2/3$ *
Fifteenth	2 *
Tierce	$1^3/5$
Mixture	III–IV
Trumpet	8 †

COUPLERS
Great to Pedal
Choir to Pedal
Choir to Great

COMPASS
Manuals: C–g^3
Pedal: C–f^1

ACTION
Tracker

CHOIR (unenclosed)	
Chimney Flute	8
Principal	4
Flute	4
Flute	2
Quint	$1^1/3$
Mixture	III
Cromorne	8 †

PEDAL	
Gedackt	16
Principal	8
Gedackt	8
Octave	4
Mixture	III
Posaune	16

ACCESSORIES
Three composition pedals to each manual
Electric and hand blowing
Transposing device
(down one semitone)

Previous organs

Lady Margaret Beaufort, Foundress of Christ's, bequeathed no fewer than three organs to the college at her death (1509). There was 'a payre of Organs the pypis of wayndskott', a 'lesser payre' with pipes of 'Tynne', and 'an olde payre with an olde case'. Possibly one of these was set up in the new chapel, for in the year following the Lady Margaret's death, the college paid for mending the organs. In 1530 'Byttn' (probably William Beton, organ maker of King's Lynn) appears in the college accounts, and in 1532–3 he received £8 'for ye residew of hys bargen of ye newe orgayns'.

How Beton's organ fared during the upheavals of the Reformation is unknown. By 1636 it was reported to Archbishop Laud that 'of the Organ (which they had) there is nothing left but a broken case'. Perhaps stimulated by the Archbishop's proposed visitation of the University the college acquired a new organ in 1636–7, when the accounts record payments 'for wood for the Organ', for carpenter's work for the organ loft, and for the 'organist' (possibly, organ-builder). By 1641 it could be reported that 'in theire singinge of hymnes and anthemes they use organs & sing alternatim'.

Shortly afterwards the organ must have been removed (the accounts for 1639–45 are missing) but, unusually, a payment of £2 is found in 1650 for 'mending the organ pipes & putting them in tune'. 'Andrews' was paid 2s 4d for mending the organ in 1652/3, and in 1655 'the Organist' received £1 10s 'for mending ye Organ ... for a frame for ye Lead Bukram, Leather, and boy to attend'. Whether these entries refer to the old chapel organ, now re-erected elsewhere, or to another domestic instrument is not apparent. To add to the confusion, in September 1658 'Mr Thamur the Organist' received £5 'towards ye setting up of the organ in ye Parlour', followed by £6 in November, and £16 17s ('more for setting up ye Organ') at the end of December. Was this the chapel organ? A clue is found in a memoir penned by Dr John Covel (Master, 1688–1723), who recalled hearing that the old chapel organ was set up in the Combination Room during the Interregnum, and that when it was returned to the chapel *c.*1660, 'ye little Organ, which before stood in ye Masters private Parlor' was moved into the Combination Room. It therefore seems likely that the expenditure of 1650–5 was on an existing organ in the Master's Lodge, and that Thamer's work in 1658 concerned the old chapel organ. Some confirmation that there were two instruments is provided by the fact that Thamer received £1 in 1659 'for keeping ye Organs'.

He seems to have moved the organ back into the chapel in 1661. The accounts for that year record the payment of £17 8s 6d to Thamer 'for setting up ye Organ', £10 14s to 'Austin ye Joyner for work about ye Organ', and £4 to Ivory 'for guilding the organs'. Interestingly, 'Mr Peas' was paid £3 10s for work on the Parlour organ shortly after this (was Thamer out of Cambridge?).

Drawing by H. T. Lilley (c.1926) of the organ in Christ's College Chapel as it appeared before 1909. Charles Quarles supplied this organ in 1705.

Right:
The organ in Christ's College after rebuilding by Bishop & Son in 1983.

Inset below:
The organ as it appeared in 1975, with extended casework added to accommodate the Norman & Beard organ of 1909.

Thamer received further small sums for tuning and repairing both organs over the next twenty years – the last payment seems to have been in 1684. Following his death, Henry Smart was paid 3s in 1688 and William Preston £2 for one week's work in 1689, and then in 1694 Renatus Harris appeared for the first time as tuner at a salary of £3 per annum.

Charles Quarles supplied a new organ in 1705; the accounts record a payment of £1 1s 6d to the musicians when it was opened on 14 April. Quarles's rôle is obscure. The surviving pipework has markings of the type associated with Bernard Smith's workshop, and the style of the case hints at the same builder. Possibly Quarles got hold of a secondhand organ, or perhaps Smith supplied him with materials. Whatever the truth, Quarles was not finally paid until August 1707 (a total of £140).

The organ stood in the present gallery on the north side of the chapel. It had an eight-stop Great and a Chair Organ with two stops. Both were housed in the handsome, three-towered case. Quarles was retained as 'organ keeper' until 1714. By 1718, he had been succeeded by Henry Turner. Turner was probably the 'organ maker' who was paid in January of that year 'for mending the great iron to raise the bellows', and also 'for removing the rats dung, and mending many pipes eaten by them and putting the whole organ in repair and driving the rats away'. The only addition to the instrument before it fell into disuse after 1785 seems to have been made in 1733, when Barnard Turner (who was also organist) completed the Trumpet stop in return for £8 'and the organ in the parlor'.

In 1865 the Master and Fellows resolved to restore the chapel organ, entrusting the work to Hill & Son. New keyboards of modern compass were provided, together with a small Swell Organ from tenor c and a two-stop Pedal Organ. Otherwise, Hill's work was conservative. The existing pipework (previously stored away at the instigation of Sir John Sutton) was retained, with the exception of the Cornet and Trumpet. The stop knobs were set in the case front so as to preserve the dimensions of the original console opening and the case itself was unaltered.

Norman & Beard rebuilt the organ in 1909, more than doubling it in size, and necessitating major alterations to the case. The upper portion was raised slightly and corbelled out over the new console. Wings were added to conceal pipework. The returns of the central tower were cut away to accommodate a Tuba. There were 36 stops (some of them 'prepared for' in 1909 and inserted in 1912) and the whole instrument was placed on tubular-pneumatic action.

Christ's College Archives: Accounts 1622–92
BL: Harleian MS 7019, f.84
JWD: 188–9
W&C, vol. 2: 207–8
BOA: Hill, Norman & Beard Archive – Hill Estimate Book 2 (1862–77): 13
Malcolm Hallowes, 'Some Cambridge college organs', in *Musical Opinion*, vol. 44 (June 1921): 775
B.B. Edmonds, 'Organs in Christ's College, Cambridge', in *The Organ*, vol. 16 (1936): 12–18
H. Rackham (editor), *Christ's College in Former Days*, (Cambridge 1939): 229–43
O&A: 43

CHURCHILL COLLEGE CHAPEL — Storey's Way

The organ was built by E. J. Johnson & Son in 1973, utilising the extension principle (from six ranks, plus a cornet, labelled A–F below). There is no case, and the pipes stand in an exposed position against the wall of the chapel.

MANUAL I (lower)

Rohr Flute	8	F
Stopped Flute	4	G
Gemshorn	4	D
Principal	2	E
Quint	$1^1/_3$	D
Cornet	III	C
Trompette	8	B

PEDAL

Subbass	16	G
Flute	8	F
Gemshorn	4	D
Mixture	II	D/E
Fagotto	16	A
Trompette	8	B
Schalmei	4	A

MANUAL II (upper)

Gemshorn	8	D
Gedeckt	8	G
Rohr Flute	4	F
Gemshorn	2	D
Mixture	II	E
Fagot	8	A

COUPLERS

Manual II to Manual I
Manual I to Pedal
Manual II to Pedal

COMPASS

Manuals: C–g^3
Pedal: C–f^1

ACTION

Electric

CLARE COLLEGE CHAPEL — Trinity Lane

The organ was built by Rudolf von Beckerath of Hamburg in 1971. A new combination system and additional accessories were installed by N.P. Mander Ltd in 1988. In 2003 Hans-Ulrich Erbslöh replaced the combination system and added two new stops (*).

GREAT	
Principal	8
Rohrflöte	8
Octave	4
Blockflöte	4
Nasat	$2^2/3$
Flachflöte	2
Mixtur	V
Trumpet	8

PEDAL	
Unterbass	16
Octave	8
Gedackt (*)	8
Choralflöte	4
Rauschpfeife	IV
Fagott	16
Schalmei	4

ACTION
Manuals and pedals: tracker
Stops: electric

SWELL	
Holzgedackt	8
Gamba (*)	8
Principal	4
Rohrflöte	4
Octave	2
Quint	$1^1/3$
Sesquialtera	II
Scharff	IV
Bärpfeife	8
Tremolo	

COUPLERS
Great to Pedal
Swell to Pedal
Swell to Great

COMPASS
Manuals: C–g^3
Pedal: C–g^1

ACCESSORIES
Six pistons each to Great and Swell
Six toe pistons to Pedal
Ten general pistons (4000 changes)
reversible toe pistons: Swell to Great, Great to Pedal, Swell to Pedal
Great and Pedal pistons coupled (button on stop jamb)
Two general cancel pistons (thumb and toe)
Two sequencer forward pistons (thumb and toe)
One sequencer backwards piston (thumb)

Previous organs

The present chapel was completed in 1769. There appears to have been no organ before 1871 when the Revd Dr Thomas H. Coles, Vicar of Honington in Lincolnshire, bequeathed one to the college. This instrument was Coles's own property and had been built originally by H. C. Lincoln. However it had stood since 1838 in Honington Church and the parishioners challenged the college's claim. At the Consistory Court which ensued, the evidence of Forster & Andrews (the Hull organ-builders) that Coles had commissioned them to enlarge the organ expressly to prepare it for Clare Chapel was decisive.

Left:
Clare College Chapel, the von Beckerath organ (1971).

Below:
Clare College Chapel, the organ in 1906.

Above:
The case as recast for the Harrison organ of 1911. One or two pieces of carving, and the general outline of the central portion are identifiable from the previous case, but the 1911 woodwork must have been largely new. It was subsequently stained to match the rest of the chapel woodwork.

The organ had three keyboards, pedals and mechanical action. The four-tower case was said (improbably) to be modelled on that in Birmingham Town Hall. It is not known who installed the organ at Clare, but in 1903 it was reconstructed by Norman & Beard who modified the tonal scheme and pneumaticised the pedal action at a cost of £350.

Harrison & Harrison carried out a complete rebuilding in 1911. Much of the existing pipework was retained, and the case was re-cast and extended by John Simpson, the college architect. The completed three-manual organ was fitted with tubular-pneumatic action. With two enclosed divisions and twenty-six stops it was a notable example of the multum-in-parvo schemes at which Harrison excelled.

In 1970 this instrument was bought by Mansfield Parish Church in Nottinghamshire, where (following extensive reconstruction) it was re-erected by N. P. Mander Ltd.

The chamber organ

The chamber organ that now stands in the north-east corner of the chapel was acquired by the college in 1986. A plaque above the keyboard reads 'John Snetzler / Londini Fecit 1755'.

The early history of this instrument is unknown, although it may once have been in Shaw House, Newbury. In 1906 it was sold to J. A. Fuller Maitland, the musicologist, and moved by Frederick Rothwell to his house in Kensington. Later, in 1920, Fuller Maitland had it moved to Borwick Hall, Carnforth, Lancashire. The organ was presented to St James, Heysham in 1939, but was sold to a private individual in 1970 from whom the college eventually acquired it. It was installed in the college chapel by John Budgen of Bishop & Son, Ipswich.

There is a single keyboard with a compass of GG (no GG#) to f^3. The stop names are engraved on metal plates let into the casework beside the wooden stop knobs. There are two pedals – one a shifting movement which silences the chorus registers, the other a swell pedal which operates the sliding front of the box in which the reed is enclosed. The stops are disposed either side of the keyboard:

	Hautbois [c^1]
Sesquialtra [bass]	Cornett [treble]
Principal	Fifteenth
Flute [bass]	Flute [treble]
Dulciana [bass]	Dulciana [treble]
Diapason [bass]	Diapason [treble]

Lincolnshire County Record Office: Diocese of Lincoln, Faculty Book 7, p. 423 (3 March 1871, Honington)
BOA: Hill, Norman & Beard Archive – N&B Order Book, vol. 8: 238 (1903)
A.H.R. Robinson, 'The Organs of Clare College, Cambridge', in *The Organ*, vol. 24 (1944): 49–54
Alan Barnes and Martin Renshaw, *The Life and Work of John Snetzler* (Aldershot 1994): 94
Michael Wilson, *The chamber organ in Britain, 1600–1830* (Aldershot 2001): 152–3

The Snetzler chamber organ (1755) in Clare College Chapel.

CORPUS CHRISTI COLLEGE — Trumpington Street

The organ was built in 1968 by N.P. Mander Ltd, with casework designed by Stephen Dykes Bower. In 1997 David Wells Organ Builders Ltd overhauled the instrument and renewed the electrical systems. The original combination pedals were replaced with toe pistons, and a new combination action with eight levels of memory was provided. The Swell mixture was re-composed, the resonators of the Bassoon were replaced, and one of the two original cymbelsterns was removed. Slight modifications to the voicing were undertaken by Ian Bell who had voiced and regulated the instrument in 1968.

GREAT	
Quintaton	16
Open Diapason	8
Stopped Diapason	8
Principal	4
Nason Flute	4
Twelfth	$2^2/_3$
Fifteenth	2
Full Mixture	III
Trumpet	8
Clarion	4
Mounted Cornet (f)	V

CHOIR	
Chimney Flute	8
Principal	4
Clear Flute	4
Nazard	$2^2/_3$
Block Flute	2
Tierce	$1^3/_5$
Mixture	III
Cremona	8
Trumpet (Great)	8
Clarion (Great)	4
Tremulant	

COUPLERS

Swell to Great
Choir to Great
Swell Octave
Swell to Choir
Swell to Pedal
Swell Octave to Pedal
Great to Pedal
Choir to Pedal
Choir Octave to Pedal
Great and Pedal combinations coupled
Generals on Swell toe pistons

SWELL	
Bourdon	8
Dulciana	8
Vox Angelica (A)	8
Spitz Flöte	4
Fifteenth	2
Nineteenth	$1^1/_3$
Sharp Mixture	III
Bassoon	16
Trumpet	8
Tremulant	

PEDAL	
Open Diapason	16
Subbass	16
Echo Bass (12 from Great)	16
Principal	8
Flute	8
Gemshorn	4
Mixture	IV
Fagott	16
Shawm	4

ACCESSORIES

Five adjustable pistons to each manual
Five adjustable general pistons
Three reversible pistons duplicated by toe pistons
Five toe pistons to Pedal
Setter piston
General cancel piston
Cymbelstern

COMPASS

Manuals: C–a^3
Pedal: C–g^1

ACTION

Electro-pneumatic

Previous organs

The Elizabethan chapel, begun in 1579, remained unconsecrated until the 1660s. The Bishop of Ely conducted a service of consecration in September 1662, and for the occasion the Master (Francis Wilford) and Dr Lawrence Womock bought an organ, which they had placed at the west end of the building. Described as 'a neat Small Organ wch projected a little into ye Chapel', it later fell into disuse and was removed in 1742, when it was 'judg'd rather an Eyesore than an Ornament'.

In 1855, Flight & Son of St Martin's Lane, Westminster installed an organ in William Wilkins' new chapel. The instrument had three manuals and pedals with a typical specification for the date, the only curiosity being a Nachthorn 8' in the Choir Organ. It cost £464. The case has been described as 'a dull but decent specimen of "Churchwarden Gothic" ... redeemed by good contemporary painted decoration on the gilded display pipes'.

About forty years after its installation, Miller of Cambridge redesigned the tonal scheme of the Flight organ, removing mixtures and other upperwork, and substituting a selection of the flute and string voices then popular. Finally, in 1959, Messrs Hill, Norman & Beard recast the tonal scheme with the intention of re-creating complete choruses on each manual and generally equipping the instrument to cope with the most important areas of the organ repertoire. When the generous benefaction of Aubrey Bateman enabled the college to commission a completely new organ, the much-rebuilt Flight was removed to the Methodist College, Belfast (and again rebuilt).

Robert Masters and John Lamb, *History of Corpus Christi College* (1753, repr. 1831): 210

W&C, vol. 1: 295

Michael Gillingham, 'The Chapel organs, past and present', in the programme for the Festival of Music to celebrate the opening of the new organ (October 1968).

Left:
The organ in Corpus Christi College Chapel, built in 1968 by N. P. Mander Ltd., with casework designed by S. E. Dykes-Bower.

Right:
The Flight organ (1855) as it appeared in c.*1908.*

DOWNING COLLEGE CHAPEL — Regent Street

The organ was built by J. W. Walker & Sons Ltd in 1966. It was rebuilt, with new mechanical action to the manuals and extensive tonal alterations, by Grant, Degens & Bradbeer Ltd in 1981.

GREAT	
Chimney Flute	8
Principal	4
Gemshorn	2
Mixture (19.22.26.29)	IV

PEDAL	
Bourdon	16
Spitz Flute	8
Nachthorn	4
Dulcian	16

ACTION
Manuals: tracker
Pedal: electric
Stops: electro-pneumatic

SWELL	
Stopped Diapason	8
Flute	4
Principal	2
Quint Flute	$1\frac{1}{3}$
Cornet (12.17)	II
Tremulant	

COUPLERS
Swell to Great
Swell to Pedal
Great to Pedal
Great and Pedal combinations coupled

COMPASS
Manuals: C–c^4
Pedal: C–g^1

ACCESSORIES
Three thumb pistons to each manual
Reversible thumb pistons: Swell to Great, Great to Pedal
Three composition pedals each to Swell and Pedal
One reversible pedal: Great to Pedal

Previous organ

A small tracker organ with two manuals, built by Bevington, was installed in the College Hall in 1928. This was moved to the new Chapel in 1953 by Hill, Norman & Beard. It is now in St Christopher's Church, Round Green, Luton.

EMMANUEL COLLEGE CHAPEL — St Andrew's Street

The organ is a new instrument, built in 1988 by Kenneth Jones and Associates of Bray, Ireland. The Great and Chaire cases incorporate virtually all the surviving parts of those installed *c.*1686; they have been restored to what are believed to be their original proportions. The Swell Organ and Pedal chorus stand in a compact third case sited behind the Great.

GREAT

Bourdon	16
Open Diapason	8
Stopped Diapason	8
Principal	4
Flute	4
Twelfth	$2^2/_3$
Fifteenth	2
Mixture	IV
Trumpet	8
Cornet (c^1)	V
Tremulant (and Chaire)	

CHAIRE

Stopped Diapason	8
Principal	4
Nason Flute	4
Nazard	$2^2/_3$
Fifteenth	2
Tierce	$1^3/_5$
Mixture	II
Crumhorn	8
Tremulant (and Great)	

SWELL

Bourdon	8
Salicional	8
Voix Celeste (c)	8
Gemshorn	4
Doublette	2
Mixture	III–IV
Cornopean	8
Oboe	8
Tremulant	

PEDAL

Sub-bass	16
Bourdon	16 *
Wood Principal	8
Bass Flute	8 *
Fifteenth	4 *
Flute	4 *
Mixture	III
Trombone	16

* Pedal registers in Great case, and partly derived in the bass

COMPASS

Manuals: C–a^3
Pedal: C–f^1

ACTION

Tracker, with parallel electric action to stops

COUPLERS

Swell to Great
Swell to Chaire
Chaire to Great
Great to Pedal
Swell to Pedal
Chaire to Pedal

ACCESSORIES

Six thumb pistons to each manual
Eight thumb pistons (generals)
Reversible thumb pistons: Swell to Great, Chaire to Great, Swell to Chaire, Great to Pedal, Swell to Pedal, Chaire to Pedal
One general cancel, and one setter button
Six toe pistons to Pedal, eight toe pistons (generals)
Reversible toe pistons: Swell to Great, Chaire to Great, Swell to Chaire, Great to Pedal, Swell to Pedal, Chaire to Pedal
Wind control (stop knob)

Previous organs

Emmanuel was a famously Puritan foundation, and this no doubt explains why there are no references to an organ in the old Elizabethan chapel.

The new chapel, designed by Christopher Wren, was consecrated in 1677, and at some date between then and 1686 an organ was installed in the west gallery. Reference to this is found in the college accounts where it is recorded (22 April 1686) that a total of £3.9s.4d was spent in 'entertaining Mr. Hothersall and his Lady Joice at dinner who gave the organ'. Burch Hothersall was a Fellow Commoner, with estates in Barbados, and his gift is said to have cost him £120 (or £140). Another source states that between 1684 and 1688 the rents from Archbishop Sancroft's estate 'for the repairing and Ornament of the chappel and Library' were principally spent in payments to the Organist. 'Organist' is a not uncommon misnomer for 'organ-builder' in accounts of this period, and it may be that these payments supplemented Hothersall's gift. The dinner in April 1686 probably celebrated the completion of the work.

For many years it has been assumed that Hothersall's organ came from elsewhere and consisted of parts of more than one instrument. Stylistically, the two cases suggest different builders, and the Great case does not appear to have been designed for the space in which it stands. This assumption was confirmed when the instrument was dismantled in 1987. The builders came to the conclusion that the cases incorporate parts of several different cases, together with mouldings and framings from other sources.

Above:
The organ in the 1970s, showing the shortened centre tower.

Left:
Drawing of the Emmanuel College organ, from the Sperling Notebooks (c.1850).

Right:
The organ today (2008).

It is not known who installed the original organ. Ninteeenth-century writers attributed it to 'Father' Smith, but both the design of the Chaire case and the fact that the Great soundboard had provision for quarter tones point rather to Renatus Harris. Either builder could have been a source for parts worked up into a 'new' instrument by someone else – Charles Quarles has been suggested, on the strength of his reputation as a supplier of organs, although there is no evidence for his presence in Cambridge before 1688 when he was appointed Organist of Trinity College.

The stop list of the organ noted *c.*1860 is almost certainly the original. The Great had eight registers (including a Cornet and Trumpet) and the Chaire three, controlled by stop levers in the back of the Chaire case. The compasses were GG to c^3, short octaves, and there were two diagonal bellows.

Henry Turner looked after the organ from 1720 at ten shillings per quarter. In 1748, he was succeeded by his son, Barnard (until 1776). Humphrey Argent, senior, took over in 1779, and was paid £7 per annum for 'playing and tuning'. By 1790, his son, Humphrey junior, was Organist, although the father continued to be paid for tuning until his death in 1795. Apart from the gilding of the front pipes by Mr Wiseman in 1733 at a cost of £28, and repairs in 1721 and 1758, the organ's history during the eighteenth century was uneventful.

Argent's services were discontinued in 1812. Thereafter, the organ was used less frequently, and by 1840 it had fallen into disuse. In 1871 Hill & Son restored the instrument, providing new keyboards (C-compass) and a new mechanical action, and adding a five-stop tenor-c Swell. A single Pedal stop was introduced and three registers added to the Choir.

E. W. Naylor was appointed Organist in 1898. In the same year Norman & Beard cleaned the organ and made some additions (Bourdon on the Pedal, Harmonic Flute and Gamba on the Great). They returned in 1907 to carry out a complete rebuilding. The new instrument had thirty-two stops, pneumatic action and a novel console in which the stops were controlled by buttons ('like those of electric bells') arranged in a line above the Swell keyboard. Each button was surmounted by a nameplate. The stop was brought 'on' by pressing the button and taken 'off' by pushing the nameplate. The buttons also enabled the organist to adjust a series of composition pistons. Little of the old organ survived except the two cases, although their silhouettes were preserved by placing much of the new organ in pavilions ranged across the west wall of the gallery.

In 1964 the organ was rebuilt by Hill, Norman & Beard. The action was electrified, the Chaire case was brought back into use to house a four-stop Positif Organ, and the tonal scheme was revised to give the instrument greater potential in the classical repertoire. There were forty-four stops and seventeen couplers.

Emmanuel College Archives: Accounts, 1680–90; Receipts, 1781–97

W&C, vol. 2: 709

E. W. Naylor, 'The New Organ', in, *Emmanuel College Magazine*, vol. XVII (1907–8): 28–45, 93–100

Andrew Freeman, 'The Father Smith organs at Cambridge', in *The Organ*, vol.1 (1922): 195–6

Kenneth Jones, 'The Organs of Emmanual College Chapel', in the programme for the inagural recital on the new organ, 10 November 1988

EMMANUEL UNITED REFORMED CHURCH **Trumpington Street**

The organ was built by Henry Willis in 1880 as an instrument with two manuals and pedals. It was remodelled in 1911 by Norman & Beard who installed tubular-pneumatic action, placed the Great reed on a separate chest and added an enclosed Choir Organ. Harrison & Harrison restored the Willis stop list in 1992, the only divergence being the addition of a Pedal reed.

GREAT	
Open Diapason	8
Gamba	8
Claribel Flute	8
Dulciana	8
Principal	4
Harmonic Flute	4
Fifteenth	2
Tromba	8
Clarionet	8

SWELL	
Lieblich Bourdon	16
Open Diapason	8
Lieblich Gedact	8
Salicional	8
Vox Angelica	8
Gemshorn	4
Flageolet	2
Mixture	III
Horn	8
Oboe	8

PEDAL	
Open Diapason	16
Bourdon	16
Trombone	16

COUPLERS
Swell to Great
Great to Pedal
Swell to Pedal

COMPASS
Manuals: C–g^3
Pedal: C–f^1

ACTION
Tracker

ACCESSORIES
Three composition pedals to each manual
Balanced swell pedal

FITZWILLIAM COLLEGE CHAPEL — Huntingdon Road

Fitzwilliam College boasts the newest college chapel in Cambridge. The architects were McCormac Jamieson Prichard, who also designed the organ case in consultation with Peter Collins (organ-builder) and Nicholas Thistlethwaite (consultant). The instrument was inaugurated by Stephen Cleobury in October 1992.

GREAT	
Open Diapason	8
Stopt Diapason	8
Principal	4
Fifteenth	2
Cornet	II
Mixture	III
Tremulant	
SWELL	
Chimney Flute	8
Open Flute	4
Fifteenth	2
Quint	$1^1/3$
Cremona	8
Tremulant	
PEDAL	
Subbass	16
Principal (Great)	8

COUPLERS
Swell to Great
Great to Pedal
Swell to Pedal

COMPASS
Manuals: C–a^3
Pedal: C–f^1

ACTION
Tracker

Right:
The Peter Collins organ in Fitzwilliam College Chapel, built in 1992.

GIRTON COLLEGE CHAPEL — Huntingdon Road

The new organ was installed by La Manufacture d'Orgues St-Martin SA (St-Martin, Switzerland) in 2002.

GRAND-ORGUE (I)

Bourdon	16
Montre	8
Flûte à cheminée	8
Prestant	4
Flageolet	2
Fourniture	IV–V
(extrait:	$1^{1}/_{3}$)

POSITIF (II)

Bourdon	8
Flûte à fuseaux	4
Doublette	2
Sesquialtera	II
(extrait:	$2^{2}/_{3}$)
Mixture	III
(extrait:	$1^{1}/_{3}$)
Cromorne	8
Tremblant	

RÉCIT (III)

Flûte harmonique	8
Gambe	8
Voix céleste	8
Flûte octaviante	4
Octavin	II
(extrait:	2)
Hautbois	8
Tremblant	

SOLO (IV)

Basson	16
Trompette	8
Cornet	V

PÉDALE

Soubasse	16
Principal	8
Bourdon à cheminée	8
Octave	4
Basson (Solo)	16

ACCOUPLEMENTS

IV/I, III/I, II/I, III/II

TIRASSES

IV/P, III/P, II/P, I/P

COMPASS

Manuals: C–g^3
Pedal: C–f^1

ACTION

Manuals and pedal: tracker
Stops: dual (tracker and electric)

Single registers can be 'extracted' from the mixtures as indicated

ACCESSORIES

Sequencer (512 combinations) activated by buttons set in the key cheeks and by toe pedals
Eight free combinations activated by buttons in key slip
Double combination system: one instant capture for everyday use; the other controlled by hard and floppy discs for long-term storage of registrations

Previous organs

Harrison & Harrison installed a two-manual organ with mechanical action in 1909. This instrument was rebuilt by E.J. Johnson & Son in 1974 to a specification drawn up by Dr Peter le Huray and Ann Bond. It had thirteen stops.

Right:
The new organ (2002) in Girton College Chapel.

GONVILLE & CAIUS COLLEGE CHAPEL — Trinity Street

The organ was built by Johannes Klais Orgelbau of Bonn in 1981.

GREAT	
Bourdon	16
Principal	8
Gemshorn	8
Quintade	8
Octave	4
Flute octaviante	4
Superoctave	2
Larigot	$1^1/3$
Cornet (b)	V
Mixture (19.22.26.29)	IV
Trompete	8

POSITIVE	
Rohrgedackt	8
Venezianerflöte	4
Nasard	$2^2/3$
Principal	2
Terz	$1^3/5$
Sifflet	1
Cremona	8
Tremulant	

COUPLERS

Swell to Great †
Swell to Positive †
Swell to Pedal 4' †
Swell to Pedal †
Great to Pedal
Positive to Great
Positive to Pedal
† electrical

SWELL	
Gedacktflöte	8
Salicional	8
Vox coelestis (c#)	8
Principal	4
Rohrflöte	4
Blockflöte	2
Sesquialter (12.17)	II
Mixture (26.29.33.36)	IV
Basson Hautbois	16
Trompette harmonique	8
Vox Humana	8
Tremulant	

PEDAL	
Offenbass	16
Subbass	16 *
Octave	8
Spitzflöte	8 *
Tenoroctave	4
Hintersatz (12.15.22)	III
Lieblich Posaune	16
Trompete	8 *

* registers by mechanical transmission from the Great

COMPASS

Manuals: C–c^4
Pedal: C–g^1

ACTION

Tracker to keys and pedals
Electric stop action

ACCESSORIES

Eight pistons to each manual
Eight general pistons duplicated by toe pistons
Eight toe pistons to Pedal
Reversible pistons and toe pistons to all couplers
Tutti piston
Setter piston
Cancel piston
Crescendo pedal

Right:
The organ in Gonville & Caius College Chapel built by Johannes Klais Orgelbau of Bonn in 1981.

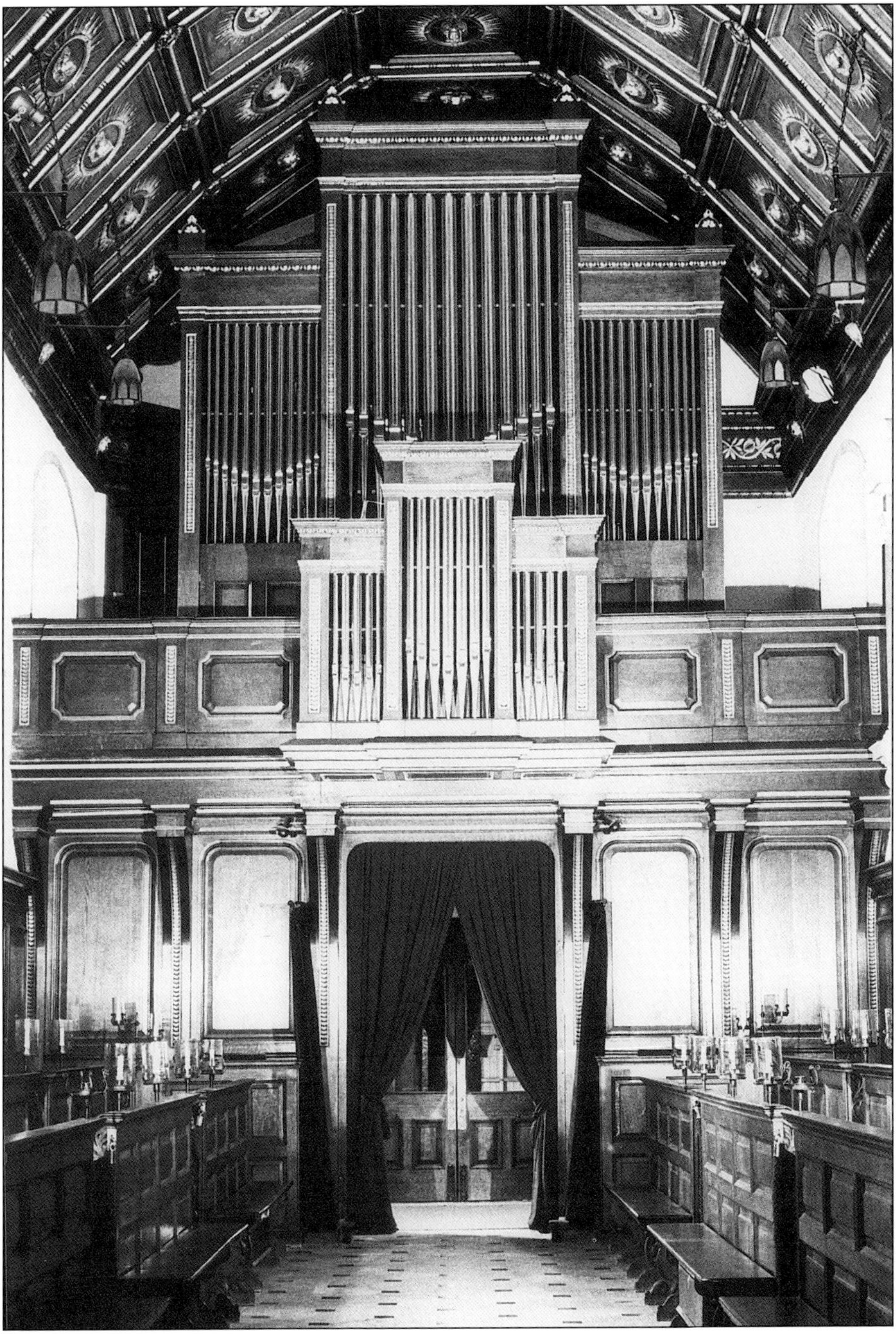

Previous organs

There may have been an organ in the mediæval chapel of Gonville Hall, but no evidence for it survives.

Following the re-foundation of the college, Dr Caius's statutes of 1573 required there to be an organ in the chapel, and stipulated that three of the scholars should be organists. Caius was a conservative figure in the increasingly radical world of Elizabethan Cambridge and it is unlikely that his wishes were fulfilled; it is, however, of interest that in 1581 a complaint was made against Caius's successor as Master, Dr Legge, that he 'used continuall and excessive loud singing and noise of organs, to the great disturbance of our studies'. Legge's music-making probably took place in the lodge rather than the chapel. The use of an organ in worship was no more than a distant memory by 1636 when it was reported to Archbishop Laud that the chapel organ had been 'long since sold away'.

In 1866 a small organ on loan from the Vicar of St Clement's was placed in the ante-chapel. Two years later, when the west gallery was built, J. W. Walker supplied a two-manual organ with fourteen stops. The same firm renovated the instrument in 1893, and in 1903 Miller added a Choir Organ and Pedal Bourdon. It was last rebuilt by Hill, Norman & Beard in 1954.

A few pipes from this organ were included in the Klais instrument. The casework was designed by Josef Schäfer and incorporates woodwork from the former organ case which itself was partly derived from the eighteenth-century reredos discarded when Waterhouse extended the chapel.

Brandon: J.W. Walker & Sons archives – Shop Book 3 (1865–72)

J. Venn, *Biographical History of Gonville & Caius College*, 7 vols (Cambridge 1897–1978), passim

Programme for the Inauguration of the new organ, November 1981: 33–37

THE GUILDHALL (The Large Hall) — Peas Hill

W. Hill & Son built a three-manual concert organ (Great, Swell, and Solo) of thirty-four stops in 1882. The same firm pneumaticised the stop action, added pistons, and undertook minor tonal modifications in 1893. In 1924 the instrument was entirely reconstructed by Hill, Norman & Beard at a cost in excess of £3,500, much of which was contributed by Mrs John Lilley Smith in memory of her late husband. The organ was opened by Dr W. G. Alcock of Salisbury Cathedral in May 1925, with a programme including pieces by Mozart, Bach, Reubke, Rachmaninoff and Lemare. Hill, Norman & Beard electrified the action in 1938.

This organ is now (2008) largely unplayable.

GREAT		
Double Open Diapason	16	A
Lieblich Bourdon	16	
Open Diapason I	8	
Open Diapason II	8	
Harmonic Claribel Flute	8	
Corno Flute	8	D
Octave	4	
Harmonic Flute	4	
Twelfth	$2^2/_3$	
Fifteenth	2	
Mixture	IV	
Posaune (in Solo box)	8	E

SOLO (enclosed)		
Gamba	8	
Harmonic Flute	8	
Celeste	8	
Lieblich Gedacht	8	
Zauber Flöte	4	
Octave Viola	4	
Dulciana Cornet	III	
Orchestral Oboe	8	
Contra Oboe	16	
Cornopean	8	
Clarinet	8	
Bassoon	16	
Tremulant		
Posaune (Great)	8	E
Tuba (unenclosed)	8	

SWELL		
Contra Viol	16	B
Open Diapason	8	
Viola	8	
Hohl Flöte	8	
Voix Celeste	8	
Octave gamba	4	
Suabe Flute	4	
Fifteenth	2	
Cornet de Violes	III	
Double Trumpet	16	
Horn	8	
Oboe	8	
Tremulant		

PEDAL		
Contra Violone	32	B
Open Diapason (wood)	16	
Open Diapason	16	A
Viola	16	B
Bourdon	16	C
Dolce	16	D
Octave	8	A
Bass Flute	8	C
Trombone (in Solo box)	16	E
Posaune (in Solo box)	8	E

Stops marked A–E are derived from extended ranks.

COUPLERS
Great pistons to Pedal pistons
Swell pistons to Pedal pistons
Great to Pedal
Solo to Pedal
Swell to Great

COMPASS
Manuals: C–c^4
Pedal: C–f^1

ACTION
Electro-pneumatic

COUPLERS (*continued*)
Solo to Great
Swell to Solo
Solo Unison off
Solo sub octave
Solo octave
Swell sub octave
Swell octave
Swell Unison off

ACCESSORIES
Five thumb pistons each to Great and Swell
Three thumb pistons to Solo
One adjustable thumb piston each to Great and Swell
Two adjustable thumb pistons to Solo
Reversible thumb pistons: Swell to Pedal, Swell to Great, Great to Pedal (2), Solo to Pedal
Five toe pistons to Pedal
One adjustable toe piston to Pedal
Reversible toe pistons: Great to Pedal, Swell to Pedal, Solo to Pedal

The Guildhall, Cambridge, following the reconstruction by Hill, Norman & Beard in 1924.

HOLY SEPULCHRE (The Round Church) — Bridge Street

There is now no pipe organ in this church.

Previous organs

A print showing the round nave before the restoration of 1841–3 reveals part of a small organ situated in a gallery at triforium level. An organist was retained in the years following the restoration but at a salary which suggests that the duties may have been restricted to turning the handle of a barrel organ.

Forster & Andrews built a new organ, probably in 1879. It was sited in the south aisle. In 1959, Hill, Norman & Beard rebuilt this instrument, relocating the pipework in the nave triforium and supplying a detached console on the north side of the chancel. Further modifications were made by E. J. Johnson & Son in 1979–80, leaving the organ with two manuals and twenty stops. It was removed during the mid-1990s when the congregation transferred to St Andrew the Great.

HOLY TRINITY CHURCH — Market Street

The present organ originated as a two-manual and pedal instrument; it had tracker action and was built by Joseph Walker in 1852. In 1879 Miller 'considerably enlarged and improved' the organ, and his work may have included removing it from the gallery position to the floor of the church. The same builder moved the organ into the new chamber on the north side of the chancel in 1891, and fitted Hope-Jones's patent electric action. Evidently this was not a success and in 1894 Bedwell of Cambridge rebuilt the organ with tracker action to the manuals and pneumatic to the pedals. Ten years later, Bedwell added a third manual and converted the whole instrument to tubular-pneumatic action. The organ was completely rebuilt by J. W. Walker & Sons Ltd in 1956.

GREAT		
Lieblich Bourdon	16	
Open Diapason No. 1	8	
Open Diapason No. 2	8	
Open Diapason No. 3	8	
Lieblich Gedeckt	8	
Salicional	8	
Principal	4	
Harmonic Flute	4	
Twelfth	$2\frac{2}{3}$	
Fifteenth	2	
Mixture	III	
Tromba	8	D

CHOIR (enclosed)		
Double Dulciana	16	E
Hohl Flute	8	
Viola	8	
Dulciana	8	E
Flauto Traverso	4	
Dulcet	4	E
Nazard	$2\frac{2}{3}$	
Piccolo	2	
Dulciana Mixture	II	E
Clarinet	8	
Tromba (Great)	8	D

Stops marked A–E are derived from extended ranks

COUPLERS
Swell to Great
Choir to Great
Swell to Choir
Choir Octave
Choir Sub Octave

SWELL		
Open Diapason	8	
Rohr Flute	8	
Viole d'orchestre	8	
Voix Celeste (c)	8	
Principal	4	
Flute	4	
Fifteenth	2	
Mixture	III	
Double Trumpet	16	
Trumpet	8	
Oboe	8	
Clarion	4	
Tremulant		

PEDAL		
Open Diapason	16	A
Bourdon	16	B
Echo Bourdon (Great)	16	
Dulciana	16	E
Octave	8	A
Bass Flute	8	B
Violoncello	8	C
Fifteenth	4	C
Octave Flute	4	B
Trombone	16	D
Trumpet (Swell)	16	
Tromba	8	D

COMPASS
Manuals: C–c^4
Pedal: C–g^1

ACTION
Electro-pneumatic

COUPLERS (*continued*)
Swell Octave
Swell Sub Octave
Great to Pedal
Swell to Pedal
Choir to Pedal
Great and Pedal
combinations coupled

ACCESSORIES
Six adjustable thumb pistons
to Great, Swell and Choir
Reversible thumb pistons:
Swell to Great
Choir to Great
Great to Pedal
Six toe pistons to Swell
(duplicating thumb pistons)
Six toe pistons to Pedal
Reversible toe piston:
Great to Pedal

The organ in Holy Trinity Church, originally built by Joseph Walker in 1852.

Previous organs

Holy Trinity Church possessed an organ at the end of the mediaeval period: in 1520 a new organ was purchased and apparently replaced an older one. It is recorded that a 'stranger' was paid 6d for playing the organ on the Feast of Corpus Christi in 1557. No doubt Puritan influence soon put a stop to that, and there was then no organ in the church until 1796 when John Lincoln of High Holborn, London installed a one-manual instrument with seven stops. H. C. Lincoln repaired his father's organ in 1820–1, and at some point Vincent added an octave of pedals. A writer commented in 1839: 'Of this instrument (except that there is not a worse in the town) nothing need be said, but that, whether it be in tune or not, whether in repair or needing it, the congregation seem equally unconscious and indifferent'.

CCRO: Holy Trinity, Cambridge – Churchwardens' Accounts, 1819–69
CGA: 22 May 1839

JESUS COLLEGE — Jesus Lane

The Main Organ

A new organ was installed in 2007. It was built by Orgelbau Kuhn of Switzerland and replaced the 1971 Mander organ.

GREAT (I)	
Bourdon	16
Open Diapason	8
Harmonic Flute	8
Stopped Diapason	8
Gamba	8
Principal	4
Flute	4
Quinte	2²/3
Fifteenth	2
Mixture	IV
Trumpet	8
Tremulant	

SWELL (II)	
Geigen Diapason	8
Lieblich Gedact	8
Salicional	8
Celeste	8
Dolce	8
Principal	4
Chimney Flute	4
Nazard	2²/3
Octave	2
Tierce	1³/5
Plein Jeu	IV
Oboe	8
Trumpet	8
Tremulant	

PEDAL (P)	
Lieblich Bourdon *	16
Subbass	16
Violone	16
Principal	8
Stopped Diapason *	8
Gamba *	8
Octave	4
Posaune	16
Trumpet *	8

* transmission from Great

COUPLERS
II–I, II–I Sub
I–P, II–P, II–P Super
Great to Pedal pistons
Generals to Swell pistons

COMPASS
Manuals: C–c⁴
Pedals: C–g¹

ACTION
Tracker to keys and pedals
Electric stop action

ACCESSORIES
Eight general pistons (199 levels)
Four 'advance' pistons in the key slips, two on the stop jambs, and two operated by toe pistons
One 'retard' piston in Great key Slip
Eight pistons each to Great and Swell (99 levels)
Reversible pistons: II–P, II–I, I–P
One general cancel piston
One setter button
Eight toe pistons each to Pedal and Swell (99 levels)
Reversible toe pistons: I–P, II–P, II–I, II–I Sub
Digital displays for general and divisional pistons, and operation of swell pedal

Above:
The new Kuhn organ (2007) in Jesus College Chapel; the console can be seen on the right, below the casework door of the Sutton organ.

Right:
The console of the Kuhn organ in Jesus College Chapel.

The Sutton Organ

This organ was the gift of (Sir) John Sutton, Fellow-Commoner of the college, and a leading member of the Cambridge Camden Society. During his years in residence (from 1845) Sutton was closely involved in the restoration of the chapel, and paid for much of the work himself; he was also responsible for recruiting a boys choir to sing choral services. Sutton admired English organs of the seventeenth century, and hoped originally to acquire an instrument by 'Father' Smith for the chapel. When this proved impossible, he commissioned J. C. Bishop, the London organ-builder, to make an instrument in the style of Smith. Five ranks of seventeenth-century pipework (marked with an asterisk in the specification) were included. The organ was installed in 1848 and opened on All Saints' Day 1849.

The case is a striking essay in ecclesiological gothic (see photograph opposite). It has often been attributed to A. W. Pugin, the architect, whose involvement in the design of the fittings for the chapel is documented. However, the original idea may have been Sutton's.

Following its extraction from the Harrison organ of 1927 (see below), the Sutton Organ was reconstructed by Noel Mander in 1967. He provided a new console on the west side of the case with a complete pedal board and a rank of pedal pipes. The original console (which had been disconnected by Harrison) survives on the east side of the organ but is no longer playable.

The college has now (2008) commissioned William Drake to restore this instrument. The organ will be returned to its nineteenth-century state, the original console will be reconnected, and the additions made in 1967 will be removed. The specification will then be:

CHOIR		ECHO	
Open Diapason	8	Open Diapason *	8
Stopt Diapason *	8	Stopt Diapason *	8
Principal	4	Principal	4
Flute *	4	Flute *	4
Twelfth	$2^2/_3$		
Fifteenth	2	PEDAL	
Sesquialtra	III	Pull-downs from Choir	

COMPASS	ACTION
Manuals: C–c^3 (49 notes)	Tracker
Pedal: C–c^1 (13 notes)	

* Seventeenth-century pipework

Previous organs

Jesus College incorporates the buildings of the former nunnery of St Radegund, founded in the twelfth century. The present college chapel was originally the conventual church, but no evidence has survived for the existence of an organ during those years.

Bishop Alcock of Ely had the nunnery suppressed in 1496 and acquired the site for his new college. The earliest statutes (1514/15) provided for choral services, including the maintenance of four youths skilled in singing, one of whom was also to act as organist. This provision was diluted in subsequent sets of statutes, and compromised by the increasingly Protestant tone of chapel

services in the Elizabethan years. The only references to an organ concern its disposal. In 1582/3 Mr Ball paid 2s 6d for '3 pypes weing fyve pounde', and Mr Lansdalle gave 6s 8d 'for the case of the Orgaines'. In the following year the destruction was completed when Robert Lawrence bought 'the rest of the organ pipes weying 28li' at 5d per pound.

The appointment of Dr William Beale as Master in 1632 signalled a change of tone. Under Beale and his successor, Richard Sterne, the college was strongly identified with the Laudian party. In October 1634, an agreement was signed with Robert Dallam for a new organ costing £200. It was completed by July 1635 and Dallam was paid an extra £12, though whether for additional work or as a token of appreciation is not recorded. A contemporary account states that the organ stood at the west end of the chapel with the letters I.H.S. (i.e., the sacred monogram) in gilt on the back. This may imply that it was on a screen. The organist's stipend was provided by charging all resident members 12d each quarter – all, that is, except the sizars, who instead were required to blow the organ. George Loosemore (later of Trinity College) was elected Organist in June 1635.

Dallam returned to tune the organ in 1638, and Henry Jennings was paid £2 5s for 'mending' in November 1641. By the time Dowsing visited the college in December 1643 it had been taken down – the accounts record a payment of 15s for the work (1642/3). The organ must have been well concealed, because an entry for the Michaelmas quarter of 1652 records a payment of £1 for 'discovery of the Organs'. A tradition that it was found buried in the Master's garden now seems to be a confusion with the fate of college plate.

Dallam's organ may have been re-erected in the chapel following the Restoration, although there is no hard evidence for this. By the mid-1660s, however, the college was turning its attention to the chapel music, and this included the renovation of the organ. In May 1665 Thomas Thamer acknowledged receipt of £60 'for making up the Organ', and the appointment of an organist was resumed in the previous month. Thamer was paid for minor work in 1669/70 and 1670/71, and an unnamed workman received £2 for mending the organ in 1679/80.

Nine shillings was spent on 'Wine at ye Opening of ye Org[an]' in 1689. Around this time, the chapel accounts record small payments 'towards ye defraying ye charge of ye organ', and it is likely that a new organ had been provided. There is no record of the maker. However, the style of the surviving case (now at Little Bardfield) suggests a possible connection with Renatus Harris's workshop, and in 1693 the college signed a tuning contract with him. Harris received £3 per annum until 1724, when Mr Turner was paid £2 10s for mending. The Turners maintained the instrument for £2 a year until 1764. The organist's salary was also discontinued in that year. By 1776 it was reported to William Cole that the instrument was deemed 'a useless Piece of Lumber and Expence', and in 1790, the Fellows resolved 'to make a present of the remains of our Organ to the Parish of All Saints in Cambridge'.

Jesus Chapel seems then to have been without an organ until the Sutton organ was opened in 1849. Sutton's taste for instruments of modest size and mellow tone was not widely shared by his contemporaries, and 40 years later, a second organ was provided for the chapel which was more in keeping with the taste of the day. This organ had four manuals and 45 stops and had been built by Norman & Beard for a private house in Norfolk. At Jesus, it was set

Jesus College Chapel, the Norman & Beard organ (1888) on the west gallery with casework designed by Bodley (c.1890). This instrument was removed in 1927.

up in a west gallery (1888) and later had a case provided for it by Bodley. The action was tubular-pneumatic, and the specification offered a wide selection of the reed, string and flute voices which were then so popular.

By 1927, the Norman & Beard organ was requiring attention. It was decided to sell it and clear the ante-chapel. The case went to St Matthew's, Portsmouth, where it was destoyed during the war, and some of the pipework was incorporated in the organ of the City Temple, Holborn Viaduct, London. Harrison & Harrison were commissioned to build a small 4-manual instrument in the gallery to the north of the Choir; two of the divisions were provided by the Sutton Organ, and Harrison added a Great, Swell and Pedal.

In 1967 this instrument was dismantled and the Sutton Organ regained its independence (see above). Four years later, N.P. Mander Ltd installed a new organ in the gallery (beside the Sutton Organ) with three keyboards and twenty-seven stops; the key and pedal actions were mechanical and electro-pneumatic action was applied to the stops. The organ was opened by Peter Hurford on 7 June 1971.

Jesus College Archives: Audit Books (1599–1764); Register (1618–89); Chapel Account (1663–1727); Articles of Agreement with Renatus Harris (1693); Conclusion Book (1790)

W&C, vol. 2: 142-4

Malcolm Hallowes, 'Some Cambridge college organs', in *Musical Opinion*, vol. 44 (May 1921): 695

Nicholas Thistlethwaite, 'The Organ of Jesus College, Cambridge, in *The Organ*, vol. 54 (1975): 1–17

A. Gray and F. Brittain, *A History of Jesus College, Cambridge* (Cambridge 1979 edn): 76, 90, 118

Ian Payne, 'Music at Jesus College, Cambridge, *c*.1557–1679', in *Proceedings of the Cambridge Antiquarian Society*, vol. 76 (1987): 97–103

C. H. Davidson, *Sir John Sutton: A Study in True Principles* (Oxford 1992)

O&A: 38–9

KING'S COLLEGE CHAPEL — King's Parade

The organ was completely rebuilt in 1934 by Harrison & Harrison Ltd, retaining the two seventeenth-century cases and much of the existing pipework. Minor work was carried out in 1950, and in 1968 several new stops (†) were introduced. Harrison & Harrison carried out further work in 1992 when the console was renovated and the electrical system modernised. The Choir Dulzian (1968) was replaced with a new Corno di Bassetto in 1997.

GREAT		SWELL	
Double Open Diapason	16	Quintatön	16
Open Diapason I	8	Open Diapason	8
Open Diapason II	8	Violin Diapason	8
Stopped Diapason	8	Voix Céleste	8
Octave	4	Lieblich Gedeckt	8
Principal	4	Echo Salicional	8
Wald Flute	4	Vox Angelica (c)	8
Octave Quint	2²/3	Principal	4
Super Octave	2	Lieblich Flute	4
Open Flute (†)	2	Fifteenth	2
Sesquialtera (17.19.22)	III	Mixture (12.17.19.22)	IV
Mixture (19.22.26.29) (†)	IV	Oboe	8
Contra Tromba*	16	*Tremulant*	
Tromba (harmonic)*	8	Double Trumpet	16
Octave Tromba (harmonic)*	4	Trumpet	8
(*) enclosed in Solo box		Clarion	4

CHOIR (enclosed)		SOLO (enclosed)	
Double Salicional	16	Contra Viola	16
(12 from Pedal)		Viole d'Orchestre	8
Open Diapason	8	Viole Octaviante	4
Claribel Flute	8	Cornet de Violes (10.12.15)	III
Salicional	8	Harmonic Flute	8
Dulciana	8	Concert Flute	4
Gemshorn	4	Cor Anglais (*)	16
Suabe Flute	4	Clarinet	8
Nazard	2²/3	Orchestral Hautboy	8
Dulcet	2	*Tremulant*	
Tierce	1³/5	French Horn	8
Larigot	1¹/3	Tuba (unenclosed)	8
Twenty-second	1	(*) extra octave of pipes for use with octave couplers	
Corno di Bassetto	8		
Contra Tromba } Great	16		
Tromba } Great	8	ACTION	
Octave Tromba } Great	4	Electro-pneumatic	

PEDAL		COUPLERS
Double Open Wood	32 A	Choir to Great
Open Wood	16 A	Swell to Great
Open Diapason (Great)	16	Solo to Great

PEDAL (*continued*)		COUPLERS (*continued*)
Geigen	16 B	Swell Octave
Bourdon	16 C	Swell Sub Octave
Salicional	16	Solo to Swell
Echo Violone (Solo)	16	Swell to Choir
Violoncello	8 B	Solo to Choir
Flute	8 C	Solo Octave
Fifteenth (from Mixture)	4	Solo Sub Octave
Rohr Flute (†)	4	Solo Unison Off
Open Flute (†)	2	Great to Solo
Mixture (12.15.17.19.22)	V	Choir to Pedal
Double Ophicleide	32 D	Great to Pedal
Ophicleide	16 D	Swell to Pedal
Trombone (Great 16′)	16	Solo to Pedal
Double Trumpet (Swell)	16	Great to Pedal foot pistons
Cor Anglais (Solo)	16	Pedal to Great pistons
Posaune	8 D	Pedal to Swell pistons
Tromba (Great 16′)	8	
Octave Tromba (Great 16′)	4	COMPASS
Schalmei (†)	4	Manuals: C–c^4
		Pedal: C–g^1

ACCESSORIES

Eight general pistons and general cancel
Two general coupler pistons
Eight foot pistons to the Pedal Organ
Eight pistons to the Choir Organ
Eight pistons to the Great Organ
Eight pistons to the Swell Organ, duplicated by foot pistons
Generals on Swell foot pistons
Six pistons to the Solo Organ
Ten reversible coupler pistons
One reversible piston to Double Ophicleide
Four reversible foot pistons to couplers
One foot piston for Doubles Off
The pistons are instantly adjustable, with eight divisional and thirty-two general memories

Previous organs

For most of the first century of its existence, the King's College of St Mary and St Nicholas was served by a chapel standing to the north of the present one. There was an organ as early as 1450–1 when the college paid 5s for repairing the 'great organs'. In 1508–9 Thomas Browne, a London organ-maker, was paid £8 for making (new?) 'great organs'. John Howe carried out repairs in 1533, and it is likely that Browne's instrument was moved to the new chapel when it was finally taken into use in 1538. Payne believes that the choir was disbanded between 1549 and 1553; this might explain why no expenditure is recorded on the organs during those years. Small payments begin again during Mary's reign, and in 1562 William Randall was paid forty shillings 'for mendynge the lesse organs'. Two years later (1564), when Queen Elizabeth visited the chapel, a *Te Deum* 'was solemnly sung in Prick Song ... the organs playing'. Where these organs stood is not recorded, but it is unlikely that they were located on the screen because the college had erected there a 'glazed closet' for the Queen's use. A few years later, in 1570, the Queen's Commissioners (perhaps under the influence of the puritan Provost Goad) ordered the removal of the organs and in the following year the college received one hundred shillings 'pro organis' and 45s 10d 'for th'old organ pipes'.

Goad was still Provost in 1603 when his opponents drew attention to the fact that the college was in default of its statutory obligations in having no organ. Between June 1605 and August 1606, Thomas Dallam was engaged in making a new instrument. It consisted of 'greate' and 'chayre' organs, housed in separate cases, and cost £371 17s 1d. The accounts have survived, and tell in detail how the college purchased the materials required by the organ-makers, and fed and boarded them for fifty-eight weeks while the work was done. Among the purchases is to be found 'tynn', 'ebony for kayes' [sc. keys], 'Ashe woodd', 'packthred to bynd the pypes', 'nayles', 'flannell clothe to laye under the kayes', 'fustian to cast the mettell uppon', 'chalke to lay upon the fustian', and 'brasse for the shaking stop' (a tremulant). A Cambridge carpenter was paid £16 for 'the frame of tymber whereon the organs [stand]', but a specialist contractor, one Hartop, was brought in to make the cases. He and his men were engaged on the job for ten months and the college paid for the carriage of his tools to and from the town. When the cases were complete they were embellished by 'Knockle the Limber' with gilding and colour. Four pipes in the Chayre and five in the Great Organ were embossed, and Knockle also gilded two stars and the '2 figures or pictures that stand in the greate Organ'.

Dallam's organ stood to the east of the choirstalls, on the site of the pre-Reformation altar. It is shown in this position on Robert Smythson's plan of *c.*1609. (The communion table was placed between the stalls – a common liturgical arrangement in the Jacobean Church.) The 'frame of tymber' may have been a low gallery or platform, intended to raise the organ above the floor. However, it had been moved to the screen by 1632–3 when the communion table was set 'altar-wise' against a new eastern screen in the third bay of the chapel. It seems likely that the move occurred as early as 1613 when Dallam was paid £30 for unspecified work 'circa Organ'. He and his men were in Cambridge for eight weeks, and (significantly) Chapman the carpenter was paid £7 10s for associated work.

The accounts record various minor repairs and tunings over the next thirty years. More substantial repairs occur in 1617 (£10) and 1635 (£22) – both by 'Dallam' (respectively, Thomas and Robert) – and in 1622 'M^ro^ Hamlin' (probably Thomas Hamlyn who worked at St James's Palace in 1613) was paid £11 13s 4d. Then, at the beginning of 1643, 'Gennynge' [sc. Jennings] was paid £2 and a joiner received £1 1s 0d for 'taking downe le Organ'. Eighteen months later, 'Ashley' was given 3s for 'taking downe the Orgaine case'.

The choral service was restored in 1660. Payments to an organ-blower commence at Michaelmas of that year, and suggest that an organ was being used within a few months of the Restoration. The college made brief use of Henry Loosemore's (the organist's) own organ, and Lancelot Pease was

Right:
The east front of the organ in King's College Chapel.

paid for moving it into the chapel and then back to Loosemore's room early in 1661. Meanwhile, Pease was making a new Chaire Organ for which he was paid £200 (a large sum) in the summer of that year. He was assisted by John Adams (carpenter) and George Woodruffe, joiner. The similarity of the King's Chaire case to that designed for Canterbury Cathedral by Pease and Woodruffe (1662) strongly suggests that it was new in 1661. Matthew Hards, one of Pease's workmen, was paid for minor repairs in 1662, and then in 1664 Thamer received £1 10s for tuning and repair. He continued to execute small repairs for the next twenty years, but undertook a major addition between 1673 and 1677 when he was paid a total of £130 for what is variously described as 'the loftier organ' and 'the new organ'. The significance is obscure (and the extended timescale is puzzling) but the most likely explanation is that Thamer provided a new Great Organ inside an existing case erected on the screen in or after 1660 (the price would not cover the cost of a new case). At the time Thamer was doing his work, Cornelius Austin was making canopies for the stalls in the chapel, and it may be that he did any necessary work on the case and provided the royal arms of Charles II which still surmount the Great case (and which must pre-date the more extensive work of 1686–7, for Charles died in 1685).

What were the origins of the case in which Thamer built his new Great Organ? It is tempting to assume that it was the Dallam case of 1605–6 which had survived the destruction of the 1640s. But is this the case shown in the Loggan print of 1690 following Renatus Harris's work? Although the receding perspective immediately suggests the work of the Dallam family (as at York Minster 1634, Quimper Cathedral, Brittany 1643–8, or St George's Chapel, Windsor Castle 1660–2) it is difficult to reconcile with some of the details in the 1605–6 accounts. For example, 'the greate pype in the middle tower' was gilded at a similar cost to each of the 'greate pypes of the owtter towers'; in other words, it was of much the same dimensions, unlike the centre pipe of the present east front. The accounts also refer to gilding both the round towers and 'the finishing or square towars' of the Great case. This implies a complex arrangement of flats and towers more like Robert Dallam's case for Magdalen College, Oxford (*c.*1632), now at Tewkesbury. It is possible, of course, that the Great case was re-cast in its present form in *c.*1660, but it is odd that the college accounts preserve no evidence for this. In its absence, it seems likely that the case in its present form dates from 1686–7, though perhaps retaining elements of an earlier case or cases.

Henry Smart repaired the organ for £2 5s in 1684, and briefly took over maintenance following Thamer's death in 1685. Then, in the summer of 1686, Renatus Harris was paid a first instalment of £100 towards the cost of a 'new organ'. This initial agreement was for £350, and the final payment was made at the beginning of 1688. A year later, Harris was paid £100 for the addition of three stops (unspecified), and £30 in 1695 for 'le trumpet stop'.

Unfortunately, nothing further is known of Harris's organ. The price is modest, and it is possible that Harris retained Pease's Chaire Organ, with modifications. The added stops may have been an Echo Organ, and if so the trumpet may have belonged there.

Right:
The Loggan print of c.1690 showing the screen and organ case in King's College Chapel.

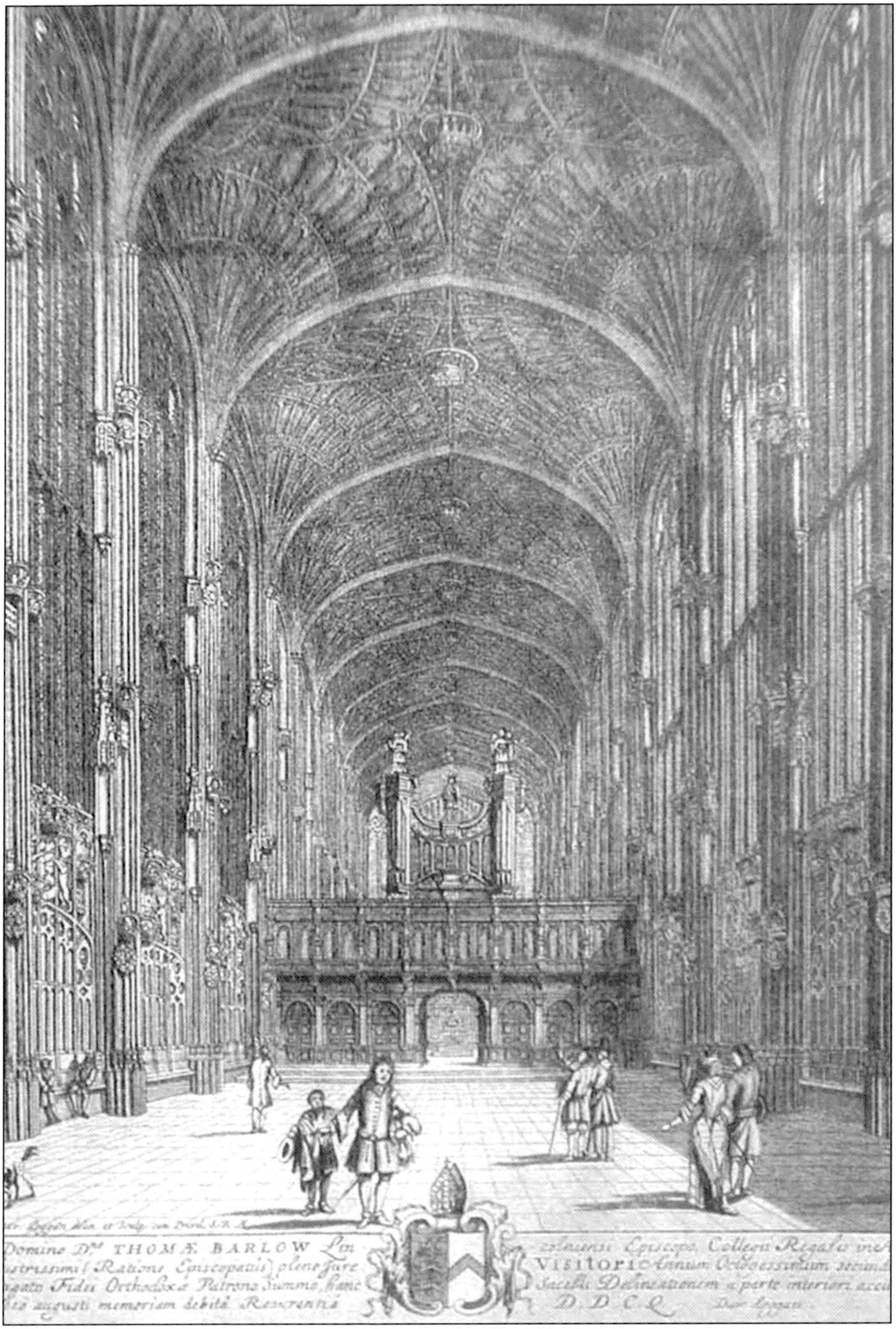
Domino Dno THOMÆ BARLOW Lin
colniensi Episcopo, Collegii Regalis
(Ratione Episcopatus) pleno Jure
VISITORI Annum Octogessimum
Fidei Orthodoxæ Patrono Summo, hanc
Sacelli Delineationem a parte interiori
augusti memoriam debitâ Reverentiâ
D. D. C. Q.

Dr A. H. Mann, organist of King's College, seated at the new four-manual console which was added by Hill in 1889: a photograph of c.1900.

Harris made a further addition in 1710 when he was paid £60 for 'le diapason=stop &c'. This probably stood partly in the east front of the Great case, the pipes of which, it was reported in 1742, were 'quite plain' and thus a contrast to the other fronts which were painted and gilded rather like the surviving fronts at Gloucester Cathedral. Harris continued to receive (erratic) annual payments for tuning (£5) until his death in 1724; by 1727, Henry Turner had taken over. In 1774, the 'plain' pipes in the east front were painted, and a month or two later it was agreed 'that the rest of the Organ also be new painted agreeably to that Range that has been painted already'. Joseph Freeman received £45 for the work. Four years later (1778), Humphrey Argent, who had succeeded Barnard Turner as tuner, was paid £35 for three new bellows and re-leathering the Choir pallets.

In April 1802 the college accepted proposals from John Avery for a new organ, and by November 1803, they had paid him £735 (including an extra £105 'in consequence of unforeseen Trouble and Expences'). Further payments totalling £121 12s 6d included £47 5s 0d for gilding the case pipes, and £21 2s 11d spent on beer 'for Mr Avery's Workmen'. The new organ had twenty-four stops, a short-compass Swell, and the first Pedal Pipes to be heard in King's – an octave-and-a-half of Unisons controlled by toe pedals. All was not well in 1805 when the Dean was authorised to 'take Measures to get the Organ put in a proper State' (the upshot is not recorded), and in 1809–10 'Mr Elliot Organ Maker' was paid £36 'for repairing and compleating the Organ left unfinished by Avery'.

William Hill first appears at King's in 1834 when he added an octave of Double Pedal Pipes (i.e., 16′ pitch) which were laid horizontally across the organ loft to the west of the Great case, and made minor tonal alterations in the Swell and Choir Organs. In 1856 he introduced pedal couplers and substituted a twenty-seven-note pedal board for the old one. The following year, Hill reported on the organ, and condemned it for 'want of vigour and point in the voicing', the lack of a Pedal Organ, the absence of 'rich toned Reed Stops and properly arranged harmonic Stops', and its generally primitive mechanism. The college commissioned him to undertake a complete reconstruction, retaining any suitable pipework, but otherwise building a modern C-compass organ. The result was a large three-manual instrument of forty-three stops, including pneumatically-assisted tracker action, a seven-stop Pedal division accommodated inside the screen, and one of the earliest hydaulic engines for raising the wind (a source of much trouble). The console was placed on the north side of the Great case, which was doubled in depth. (It was at this time that Scott reinstated the angel trumpeters on the west towers, displaced by Gothick pinnacles in 1742.)

Hill & Son overhauled the instrument in 1876 and made some tonal alterations. Twelve years later (1888) a further extensive rebuilding was planned by Thomas Hill and Dr A. H. Mann, the college organist. Tubular-pneumatic action was used throughout, and a new four-manual console was provided with splayed jambs and thumb pistons. The Great and Pedal reeds were placed on higher wind pressures than the flue choruses, the new Solo Organ included 16′ and 8′ tubas on a heavy wind, and both the Choir and Solo abounded in varieties of string and flute tone. There were fifty-five stops in all, and the organ was re-opened in February 1889 with a performance of Sterndale-Bennett's *The Woman of Samaria* and an organ

recital by Dr G.C. Martin of St Paul's Cathedral. Further alterations were made by Hill in 1911, including the revoicing of the Swell reeds on a heavier pressure and the addition of a powerful new open diapason to the Great, and in this form the instrument passed into the hands of Harrison & Harrison in 1934.

Bureau Organ

This usually stands close to the choirstalls in the chapel and is used in service accompaniment. It was built by E.J. Johnson & Son in 1971.

MANUAL		COMPASS
Gedeckt	8	Manual: C–g^3
Rohr Flote	4	
Prinzipal	2	ACTION
Terz (c)	$1^3/5$	Tracker
Mixtur	II	

King's College Archives: Mundum Books (1605–1810), Congregation Books (1722–1821), miscellaneous correspondence concerning the organ (1857–1911)
JWD: 179–80
E.J. Hopkins & E.F. Rimbault, *The Organ* (London, 1877, 3rd edition): 64–67
W&C, vol. 1: 518–21
BOA: Hill Letter Book (1838–61), Hill & Son Estimate Book (1861–77)
Dr A.H. Mann: mss in Norwich County Record Office and King's College, Rowe Music Library
Malcolm Hallowes, 'Some Cambridge college organs', in *Musical Opinion*, vol. 44 (April 1921): 611
Andrew Freeman, 'The Organs at King's College, Cambridge', in *The Organ*, vol. VIII (1929): 129–38
Ian Payne, *Provision and practice of sacred music at Cambridge ... 1547–1646* (New York and London, 1993): *passim*
Graham Chainey, 'The East End of King's College Chapel', in *Proceedings of the Cambridge Antiquarian Society*, vol. LXXXIII (1994): 141–65
Stephen Bicknell, *The History of the English Organ* (Cambridge, 1996): 74
Nicholas Thistlethwaite, 'Dr Mann and the organ of King's College, Cambridge: 1857–1912', in *JBIOS*, vol. 29 (2005): 19–44
O&A: 29–30, 34–7, 44
Nicholas Thistlethwaite, 'Boris Ord and the reconstruction of the organ in King's College, Cambridge: 1932–4', in *JBIOS*, vol. 31 (2007): 6–39
Nicholas Thistlethwaite, 'The organ of King's College, Cambridge: 1605–1802', in *JBIOS*, vol. 32 (2008): *forthcoming*

Left:
The west-facing front of the organ in King's College, photographed in 1962.

MAGDALENE COLLEGE CHAPEL — Magdalene Street

A new organ was installed in 2000. Stylistically it derives from the organs of 'Father' Smith and was made by Martin Goetze & Dominic Gwynn of Welbeck, Nottinghamshire.

GREAT	
Open Diapason	8
Stop Diapason	8
Principal	4
Flute	4
Twelfth	2^2/3
Fifteenth	2
Sesquialtera (17.19.22)	III
Mixture (26.29)	II
Trumpet	8
Vox Humana	8
Cornet (8.12.15.17)	IV

PEDAL	
Bourdon	16
Open Diapason	8
Principal	4
Trumpet	8

COMPASS
Manuals: C–g^3
Pedal: C–f^1

CHAIR	
Open Diapason	8
Stop Diapason	8
Principal	4
Nason Flute	4
Nasard	2^2/3
Fifteenth	2
Tierce	1^3/5
Mixture (22.26.29)	III
Cromhorn	8
Tremulant	

COUPLERS
Chair to Great
Great to Pedals
Chair to Pedals

ACTION
Tracker

ACCESSORIES
Thee composition pedals to Great
Three composition pedals to Chair

Previous organs

In 1677 Dr Duport gave an organ to the college, but it was in use for only a few years before the Fellows decided to dispense with the services of an organist in order to save money (1693). The organ seems to have been removed during the first half of the eighteenth century.

By the end of the nineteenth century there was a one-manual Casson Positive in the chapel which went eventually to the Bishop of Winchester's Palace at Wolvesey.

This was presumably in 1927 when the London firm of A. Hunter & Son installed a two-manual organ of 23 stops in the gallery at the west end of the chapel. It was altered by Willis in 1938 and rebuilt by Norman Hall & Sons in 1975.

W&C, vol. 2: 375
Gwilym Beechey, 'The Organ at Magdalene College, Cambridge', in *The Organ*, vol. 50 (1971): 133–136

Right:
The Goetze & Gwynn organ (2000)
in Magdalene College Chapel.

Magdalene College Chapel (c.1980) showing the Hunter organ (1927) after alteration by Willis in 1938 and rebuilding by Norman Hall & Sons in 1975. It was removed when the new Goetze & Gwynn organ was installed.

Below: Our Lady and The English Martyrs, the Abbott & Smith organ (1890) rebuilt by Johnson & Son in 1976, and by Nicholson & Co. in 2002.

OUR LADY & THE ENGLISH MARTYRS — Hills Road

The organ stands on a gallery in the south transept of the church. It was built by Abbott & Smith of Leeds in 1890 to the design of Professor C.V. Stanford. The Reverend Noel Bonavia-Hunt revoiced parts of the organ in the early years of the twentieth century in an attempt to reinforce the 'Schulze' character of the tone. E. J. Johnson & Son converted the action to electro-pneumatic in 1976, and in 2002 Nicholson & Co. Ltd (Worcester) renovated the organ, adding the Tuba and considerably extending the provision of accessories.

GREAT	
Double Diapason	16
Large Open Diapason	8
Small Open Diapason	8
Doppel Flute	8
Principal	4
Harmonic Flute	4
Fifteenth	2
Mixture (15.19.22)	III
Trumpet	8
Clarion	4

CHOIR (enclosed)	
Open Diapason	8
Dulciana	8
Clarabella	8
Violoncello	8
Lieblich Flute	4
Piccolo	2
Contra Fagotto (c)	16
Clarinet	8
Tuba (unenclosed)	8

COMPASS
Manuals: C–a^3
Pedal: C–f^1

ACTION
Electro-pneumatic

SWELL	
Bourdon	16
Open Diapason	8
Lieblich Gedeckt	8
Viola da Gamba	8
Voix Celeste (c)	8
Principal	4
Fifteenth	2
Mixture (19.22)	II
Double Trumpet	16
Horn	8
Oboe	8
Clarion	4
Tremulant	

PEDAL	
Open Diapason	16
Bourdon	16
Violoncello	8
Trombone	16

COUPLERS
Swell to Great
Swell to Choir
Swell to Pedal
Great to Pedal
Choir to Great
Choir to Pedal
Swell Super Octave

ACCESSORIES
Eight thumb pistons to Great Organ, duplicated by toe pistons
Eight thumb pistons to Swell Organ, duplicated by toe pistons
Eight thumb pistons to Choir Organ
Reversible thumb pistons to all unison couplers
Reversible toe pistons: Swell to Great, Great to Pedal
Great and Pedal combinations coupled. Generals on Swell toe pistons
Eight general thumb pistons: 96 levels of memory with 16 divisional levels
Setter piston, General cancel

Noel Bonavia-Hunt, *Irons in the Fire* (London, 1959): 83–5

The organ was built by N.P. Mander Ltd in 1980 and incorporates the cases and some pipework (indicated by an asterisk in the specification) from the instrument supplied by Charles Quarles in 1708. The consultant was Cecil Clutton.

GREAT		CHAIRE	
Open Diapason *	8	Stopped Diapason *	8
Stopped Diapason *	8	Principal *	4
Principal	4	Nason *	4
Twelfth	2 2/3	Fifteenth	2
Recorder	2	Cymbal	III
Tierce	1 3/5	Vox Humana	8
Furniture	IV		
Trumpet	8	PEDAL	
Cornet (c¹)	V	Bourdon	16
		Principal	8
COUPLERS		Fifteenth	4
Chaire to Great		Mixture	IV
Great to Pedal		Bass Shawm	16
Chaire to Pedal		Trumpet	8

ACCESSORIES	COMPASS
Great to Pedal (by pedal)	Manuals: AA, C–g^3
Chaire to Great (by pedal)	Pedal: C–f^1
Tremulant (affects all departments)	
	ACTION
	Tracker

Previous organs

References to organs are scanty. A payment made 'Pro [le] Organ Player' in 1470 may be evidence of the existence of an organ, or it may refer to some itinerant entertainment. The college possessed an organ in the following century, but this only emerges because it was sold for 33s 4d in 1567.

Nothing more is heard of organs until the 1630s. Under the Mastership of Benjamin Lany the chapel was 'beautified' and the 1641 report into 'Innovations in Religion' notes that 'Organs with anthemes are used insteed of ye singing psalmes'. Lany was evidently responsible for this, but nothing is known of the source of the organ or the date of its introduction.

The records are silent as to the fate of this instrument. Nor is it known whether the college was served by an organ during the years immediately following the Restoration. The building of a new chapel in 1665 would have imposed a strain on the college's finances, and there is no mention of an instrument until 1675, when it was ordered that 'an Organ be made for ye New chappell'. The Master, the Dean, and the 'Book keeper for ye Chappell'

Right:
The organ in Pembroke College Chapel.

Left:
Framlingham, Suffolk, the organ by Thamer (1675) which was removed from Pembroke College Chapel, Cambridge in 1708.

Right:
Drawing of the Pembroke College organ, from the Sperling Notebooks (c.1850)

were admonished to take care 'to agree with Mr Thamar about ye price of it & all things els concerning ye setting of it up'. The price turned out to be £210. The order implies that a completely new organ was provided by Thamer (as does the price), although there remains a slight possibility that an older case was used.

Thamer returned to clean the organ in 1682–3 for £1 10s. Preston undertook work totalling £31 12s 1½d in 1691–2 and 1693–4, and Renatus Harris had charge of the organ from then until 1707.

In that year, the college concluded an agreement with Charles Quarles to supply 'A Double Organ in two distinct cases' and to remove Thamer's organ to the college living of Framlingham in Suffolk where the case and some pipework survive. Quarles' organ was to have Great and Chair Organs with a total of eleven stops, and provision was made for the addition of a trumpet. Interestingly, the cost was virtually the same as Thamer's organ – £210 10s, of which the college paid £60 on signing the agreement and the remainder by annual instalments of £21 10s.

Quarles was organist of Trinity College (1688–1717). Little is known of his organ-building activities, but it is doubtful whether he actually made the organs he supplied. The Pembroke organ includes pipework which probably came from the workshop of Bernard Smith, and this suggests either that Quarles was an entrepreneur, or that he acquired and used up secondhand materials.

A flute stop (Chair) and trumpet (Great) were added by Quarles in 1711–12, but the organ did not give satisfaction. In 1719, Abraham Jordan was paid the substantial sum of £80 for 'repairing and completely finishing' the chapel organ. He received a further £8 in 1730–1. Thereafter, the organ passed into the care of the Turners, Henry and Barnard, until the latter's death in 1776. According to Cole, the organ was 'laid aside ... tho' a fine instrument, in 1779'.

It remained silent until the 1860s. In 1864, William Hill restored the instrument at a cost of £200, and in 1872 his son Thomas undertook a more extensive rebuilding which included the provision of Swell and Pedal divisions, new bellows and the renewal of the Choir action. Further work in 1881 involved moving the main case back a little, the provision of new keyboards and the introduction of hydraulic blowing.

Norman & Beard rebuilt the organ in 1902: the pipework was revoiced, new registers were added, a modern console was provided and the whole organ was equipped with tubular-pneumatic action. There were 30 stops and the work cost £581. In 1954, Hill, Norman & Beard converted the action to electro-pneumatic and installed a new console. Only minor changes were made to the stop list. This instrument was dismantled in 1977 when the gallery was found to be unsafe.

Pembroke College Archives: College Register; Hardwick Accounts
BL: Harleian MS 7019, f.81
JWD: 161–2
BOA: Hill, Norman & Beard Archives – Hill Estimate Book 2 (1862–77) and Shop Book 2 (1875–83); Norman & Beard Order Book 8 (1902–3)
Ian Payne, 'Music at Jesus College, Cambridge, c.1557–1679' [*sic*] in *Proceedings of the Cambridge Antiquarian Society*, vol. 76 (1987): 102–3

PETERHOUSE CHAPEL — Trumpington Street

The case and much of the pipework date from Snetzler's organ of 1765. The instrument was last rebuilt in 1963 by Noel Mander, who enlarged it by adding several extension ranks (indicated by A–E below).

GREAT			SWELL		
Open Diapason (S)	8		Salicional	8	
Stopt Diapason	8		Stopt Diapason (S)	8	
Principal (S)	4		Principal (S)	4	
Nason Flute	4		Fifteenth	2	
Twelfth (S)	$2^2/_3$		Mixture	III	
Fifteenth (S)	2		Oboe	8	
Mixture	II				
Trumpet	8	A	PEDAL		
			Open Diapason	16	D
CHOIR			Bourdon	16	E
Echo Dulciana (S)	8		Octave	8	D
Stopt Diapason (S)	8		Flute	8	E
Flute (S)	4		Fifteenth	4	D
Principal (S)	4		Flute	4	E
Gemshorn	4	B	Trombone	16	A
Nazard	$2^2/_3$	C	Trumpet	8	A
Gemshorn	2	B	Clarion	4	A
Tierce	$1^3/_5$				
Larigot	$1^1/_3$	C	COUPLERS		
Trumpet	8	A	Swell to Great		
			Swell to Choir		
COMPASS			Swell to Pedal		
Manuals: C–g^3			Great to Pedal		
Pedal: C–f^1			Choir to Pedal		

ACCESSORIES

Five thumb pistons to each manual
Five toe pistons each to Pedal and Swell
Three reversible thumb pistons: Great to Pedal; Swell to Great; Choir to Pedal
Three toe pistons, duplicating reversible thumb pistons

ACTION

Tracker action to manual soundboards
Electro-pneumatic stop action
Electric action to unit chests

(S) = wholly or partly by Snetzler

Right:
Peterhouse Chapel, the Snetzler organ (1765) following restoration by N. P. Mander Ltd in 1963.

DONO

Previous organs

Peterhouse Chapel is one of the most potent expressions of Laudianism in the University. It was built between 1628 and 1632 during the mastership of Matthew Wren, although many of the furnishings were acquired under his successor, John Cosin. Both were staunch allies of William Laud. A contemporary account of the expenses records that £140 was spent on an organ. It may have been installed in time for the chapel's consecration (1632), or possibly in 1635 when £4 4s 1d was allowed for two journeys to Doddington in the Isle of Ely 'circa organum'. A list of desiderata includes the embellishment ('ornatus') of the organ, implying that as originally installed the organ case was plain.

There seems also to have been a second organ, given by John and Alicia Peyton, friends of Cosin, in order 'that the Scholars might practise sacred music in the Parlour'. It was valued at £40.

Peterhouse was notorious among the Puritan faction for its 'popish superstitious practises'. The chapel organ would have played its part in the choral services which flourished briefly during the years preceding the Civil War, and to which the surviving Peterhouse part-books bear witness. When the Puritans gained the upper hand, the organ and other chapel furnishings were speedily hidden away in the Library, Anthony Fawkner being paid 9s 6d on 23 April 1643 'for worke about the frames for the blew hanging done in the Chapple & remooving the organ pipes'. A few years later, the new Master got wind of this and ordered the Library to be searched. The substantial haul included altar cloths, carpets and hangings, and also 'The Organ Pipes of Wood & Mettall'. In July 1650 it was decided to sell some of the items 'to the best advantage of the colledge'. The organ was sold for £31 to Mr Gregory Hardwick, a citizen of London. 'Mr Peas' (presumably Lancelot Pease) took the organ, together with 'the remaining pipes of Our Hall Organ' (was this the Peyton instrument?) to London and set it up there. When the Prayer Book was restored in 1660 the college attempted to recover the organ from Hardwick, first 'in a friendly way', and then by initiating a legal action, but it is a measure of their success that in 1666 the chapel was 'not yet provided of an Organ, nor of more money than £25 towards ye Purchase of one'. Giving up hope, the Fellows resolved to buy a new instrument. Mr Ashburnham donated £20 (1666–7) and the accounts record a further £44 for 'Expensae circa Organum' (1667–8). It was to have been ready by Michaelmas 1666 but was delayed 'by reason of ye Plague in ye Town'. However, on 12 March 1667, Thomas Thamer gave the Senior Bursar a receipt for £20 'in full for my work & materials, about the Organ in ye Chapell', and thus established both the builder and the date of completion. In the same year the first post-Restoration organist appears, regrettably unnamed. A former Master, Dr Bernard Hale, who died in 1663, had left an endowment for eight scholars and an organist; from 1666–7, the accounts record a regular annual payment of £26 13 4d to the latter. The sum of £2 11s was expended on the organ in 1670–71, and an annual payment of £1 10s (surely for tuning) begins in 1673–4. Nothing further is known about this instrument, although it is likely to be the organ whose existence was noted by Blomefield in 1750.

In 1765, Horatio Mann, Fellow Commoner of Peterhouse, donated a new organ. The builder was John Snetzler – a Swiss organ-maker who had settled in London during the 1740s. He provided a two-manual instrument with nine stops on the Great (including a mounted cornet) and a second manual consisting of a combined Choir and Swell, each with four stops. The handsome case is typical of Snetzler's style, especially the lower pipe flats. Avery added a few unison (8') Pedal pipes in 1804 and Elliott & Hill a manual coupler in 1830. In 1852 Hill replaced Avery's rudimentary toe pedals with a 'German' pedal board of 27 notes and added a rank of 16' open wood pipes. He also provided a new bass to the Great trumpet (Snetzler's had been a clarion bass) and cleaned the organ at a total cost of £150.

Hill & Son returned in 1893–4 to carry out a conservative rebuilding retaining the 'old black keys' and most of Snetzler's pipes. The Swell was rebuilt on modern lines with a keyboard (also with 'reversed' colours) to itself, the compasses were reduced to C, and a two further Pedal stops were added. It cost £350.

Peterhouse Archives: Account Rolls; Hale Estate Accounts, 1663–1734; correspondence concerning recovery of organ, 1660–1; miscellaneous vouchers (chapel)
BL: Harleian MS 7019, f.71
JWD: 155–59
Francis Blomefield, *Collectanea Cantabrigiensia* (Norwich 1750): 155, 157
BOA: Hill, Norman & Beard Archive – Elliott & Hill partnership Account (1827–32); Hill Letter Book (1838–61)
W&C, vol. 1: 42–3, 47
W. E. Dickson, 'Old Times in Cambridge', *Musical Opinion*, vol. 16 (1893): 398
Thomas A. Walker, *Peterhouse* (Cambridge 1935): 57, 127–9
Ian Payne, *Provision and practice of sacred music at Cambridge … 1547–1646* (New York and London, 1993): 93–100
O&A: 38, 42

QUEENS' COLLEGE CHAPEL — Queens' Lane

The present organ was installed in Bodley & Garner's new Chapel in 1892. The case is by G. F. Bodley, and the instrument was built by James J. Binns of Bramley, Leeds. E. J. Johnson & Son electrified the actions in 1965. In 2002 Harrison & Harrison undertook a further overhaul and renewed all the electrical components.

GREAT	
Bourdon	16
Open Diapason	8
Viola	8
Hohl Flöte	8
Octave Diapason	4
Flute Harmonique	4
Nazard	$2^2/_3$
Doublette	2
Mixture	III
Posaune	8

CHOIR (enclosed)	
Salicional	8
Dolce	8
Gedact	8
Flauto Traverso	4
Flautina	2
Orchestral Oboe	8
Corno di Bassetto	8
Tremulant	

COUPLERS

Great to Pedal
Swell to Pedal
Choir to Pedal
Swell to Choir
Choir to Great
Choir Octave
Swell to Great
Swell to Great Sub Octave
Swell to Great Octave
Swell Sub Octave
Swell Octave
Great and Pedal combinations coupled
Generals on Swell foot pistons

ACCESSORIES

Continued overleaf

SWELL	
Lieblich Bourdon	16
Geigen Principal	8
Viol d'Orchestre	8
Lieblich Gedact	8
Voix Celestes	8
Salicet	4
Suabe Flute	4
Mixture	III
Cornopean	8
Oboe	8
Tremulant	

PEDAL	
Contre Basse	16
Sub Bass	16
Quint (from Sub Bass)	$10^2/_3$
Octave (from Contre B.)	8
Flute Bass (from Sub Bass)	8

COMPASS

Manuals: C–c^4
Pedal: C–f^1

ACTION

Electro-pneumatic

*Right:
The organ in Queens' College Chapel with casework designed by Bodley in 1892.*

Alleluia
Alleluia
Lauda Sion Salvatorem in Hymnis

ACCESSORIES
Eight general thumb pistons
Six thumb pistons each to Great, Swell and Choir
Reversible thumb pistons: Swell to Great, Choir to Great, Swell to Choir, Great to Pedal, Swell to Pedal, Choir to Pedal
Six toe pistons to Pedal
Six toe pistons to Swell
Reversible toe pistons: Great to Pedal, Swell to Great
Two adjustable toe pistons
Twenty-five piston memories
General cancel

Previous organs

The former college chapel in Front Court (now part of the Library) housed at least four organs at different periods, but information concerning them is scanty.

In 1570 'Thomas ye virginall maker' was paid 3s 4d for 'taking down thorgans' – no doubt a symptom of increasing Puritan influence in the college. However, sixty years later, Laud's former Chaplain, Edward Martin, became President, and Queens' became one of the more ritually 'advanced' colleges in the university. The chapel was repaired, and in 1637 £114 8s 1d was found 'for the Organs'. Later that year, the 'Organ wheele' was mended, and in November John King was paid 'for 2 brasen pulliss for ye Organ'. The following month Henry Jennings received 15s for cleaning and tuning, and in February 1638 a joiner was paid for 'ye Cover over ye Organ' (to protect it while other work was going on?). By 1641 a choir had been formed, and it was reported that 'anthems are used insted of singing of psalmes with ye Organs'. The final reference to the chapel organ was in October 1642, when rails were provided for the stairs to the chamber 'next ye Organs'. No record has been found of its demolition, but it had probably gone by the time Dowsing visited the college in December 1643 – he makes no mention of it.

A new organ was provided or an old one reinstated after the Restoration. The earliest reference to it is found in June 1665 when the 'Organ mender' was paid £2.10s. Thamer received £2 for repairs in 1676 and a further £1 in 1679. Payments for blowing the organ are found in 1689, 1704 and 1708, but there are no further mentions until July 1710 when the cook was granted £2 6s 3d for 'exceedings at opening ye new Organ'. The cost of making this 'intire new Organ in ye Chappell' was £164 6s 10½d but no maker is named.

It is not clear where this organ stood, but in 1740 an organ chamber was created by converting some rooms on the north side of the chapel; there was a vestry underneath. Writing in 1742, Cole noted:

> ... over this [vestry] door stands ye organ loft supported by two Iron Pillars in ye Chapel; and ye Organ, wch is a very handsome one, stands sideways in ye North Wall of ye chapel ...

The effect must have been similar to Christ's.

By 1768 the organ had been removed from its gallery to make way for a pew for the President. William Fortrey, Esquire of Norton by Galby in Leicestershire bought the instrument, and it was rebuilt (where is not known) by

Thomas Parker, the London organ-builder.* Payments to a college organist had ceased in 1726, so it would seem that the college decided to dispense with the organ as well as the player. It would appear, however, that at some date subsequent to this another instrument found its way into the chapel, because a writer describing the interior prior to Bodley's work of 1858–61 commented upon the survival of 'a very quaint organ ... of the Jacobean period' against the north wall. Nothing is known of its fate. Perhaps it was an old chamber organ.

Bodley created a new organ chamber on the south side of the chapel and an organ (almost certainly a new instrument) was placed there. It was rebuilt by Nicholson's of Worcester in 1886, and was presumably disposed of when the new chapel was built shortly afterwards.

Queens' College Archives: Journale, vols. 6 & 7 (1621–1753); Bursar's Books (1688–9, 1716–86)
BL: Harleian MS 7019, f.78
Lincoln Cathedral Archives: A/4/14(e) – Memorandum on Thomas Parker, unsigned, *c.*1767
W&C, vol. 2: 37, 40–43
John Twigg, *A History of Queens' College, Cambridge* (Bury St Edmunds, 1987)
Ian Payne, *The provision and practice of sacred music at Cambridge ... 1547–1646* (New York & London, 1993): 105–6
O&A: 37, 43

(*) It is possible that Fortrey had the organ erected either in Galby Church or his new 'Gothick' church at King's Norton. It does not now survive in either place, but there is an organ front of *c.*1700 at nearby Great Bowden with marked 'Cambridge' characteristics, and it is at least possible that this is the former Queens' case.

RIDLEY HALL CHAPEL — Ridley Hall Road

The organ was built in 1903 by Norman & Beard. In 1983, Norman Hall & Sons electrified the action and made some tonal changes.

GREAT	
Open Diapason	8
Wald Flute	8
Principal	4
Fifteenth	2

SWELL	
Lieblich Gedeckt	8
Geigen Principal	4
Flageolet	2
Hautboy	8

PEDAL	
Bourdon	16
Bass Flute	8
Choral Bass	4

COUPLERS

Swell to Great
Great to Pedal
Swell to Pedal
Swell Octave

ACCESSORIES

Three thumb pistons each to Great and Swell
One reversible piston, Great to Pedal
One general cancel

COMPASS

Manuals: C–a^3
Pedal: C–f^1

ACTION

Electro-pneumatic (some pedal direct electric)

ROBINSON COLLEGE — Grange Road

The organ was built by Th. Frobenius & Sønner (Denmark) and opened by Gerald Gifford, the consultant, on 2 May 1981. The casework was designed by Gillespie, Kidd & Coia (architects to the college) in consultation with Walter Frobenius and Gerald Gifford.

GREAT		SWELL	
Principal	8	Gedakt	8
Fløjte	8	Gamba	8
Oktav	4	Principal	4
Fløjte	4	Fløjte	4
Quint	$2^2/3$	Nasard	$2^2/3$
Oktav	2	Oktav	2
Blokfløjte	2	Larigot	$1^1/3$
Terts	$1^3/5$	Scharf	III
Mixtur	IV	Krumhorn	8
Trompet	8	*Tremulant*	
Tremulant			

PEDAL	
Subbass	16
Oktav	8
Gedakt	8
Superoktav	4
Mixtur	III
Fagot	16
Skalmej	4

COUPLERS
Swell to Great
Swell to Pedal
Great to Pedal
Great and Pedal combinations coupled

COMPASS
Manuals: C–c^4
Pedal: C–g^1

ACCESSORIES
Four thumb pistons each to Great, Swell, and Pedal
Four thumb pistons (generals)
Four toe pistons to Pedal
Four toe pistons (generals)
Reversible thumb pistons: Great to Pedal, Swell to Pedal, Swell to Great
Reversible toe pistons: Great to Pedal, Swell to Pedal, Swell to Great
General cancel piston
Adjustable tremulants

ACTION
Key and pedal actions: tracker
Stop and combination actions: electric

The church was closed for worship during the 1970s. In 1993 it was brought back into use by the congregation of Holy Sepulchre (The Round Church). Most of the existing furnishings were removed at this time and there is now no pipe organ in the building.

Previous organs

Thomas Elliot built an organ with one manual and six stops in 1810. In 1842 the old church was demolished and a new church was built to the designs of Ambrose Poynter. G.M. Holdich provided a two-manual organ in 1844; it stood in the west gallery and was described by Sperling as 'a very good organ'. Minor additions were made by Miller (1873) and Hill (1882), and then in 1904 Hill & Son undertook a major rebuilding in the course of which the organ was re-sited in the south-east corner of the building. It had three manuals, twenty-seven stops and tubular-pneumatic action throughout. Hill, Norman & Beard made minor modifications in 1931.

Following the redevelopment of the church in the 1990s the pipework of the organ was acquired by Chelmsford Cathedral, where it forms the basis of the chancel organ built by N.P. Mander Ltd in 1995.

CCRO: St Andrew the Great archives, including – Holdich's estimate (1843) and invoice (1844); Miller's estimate (1873)
Sperling Notebooks (RCO/BL), vol. 2: 34
BOA: Hill, Norman & Beard Archive – Hill Order Books (1882, 1904); Hill, Norman & Beard Order Book (1931)

Right: St Andrew the Great in c.1896 showing the organ as it appeared before its removal from the west gallery in 1904.

Left: Robinson College Chapel, organ built be Th. Frobenius & Sønner, Denmark, in 1981.

ST ANDREW THE LESS (The Abbey Church) — Newmarket Road

It is not known who built this instrument or when it was built. The neat little case with its wing doors and embossed centre pipe suggests Sutton's influence – it is similar to a case in Belgium designed by Jean de Béthune, a friend and collaborator of Sutton. The church was restored under the supervision of the Cambridge Architectural Society (represented by the Revd John Gibson, another of Sutton's circle) in 1854–6 and it is likely that the organ was installed at this time. The console bears A. T. Miller's plate. As his business was not established until 1856 this could be his earliest extant instrument. The original Twelfth has been displaced by a Dulciana (possibly in 1924 when unspecified work was carried out) and the organ was overhauled during the 1960s.

MANUAL

Open Diapason	8
Stop Diapason bass (12)	8
Stop Diapason treble	8
Gamba (c)	8
Dulciana (c)	8
Principal	4
Flute	4
Fifteenth	2

PEDAL

Bourdon	16

COUPLER

Manual to Pedal

COMPASS

Manual: C–g^3

Pedal: C–a [*sic*]

ACTION

Tracker

Previous organ

Until the building of Christ Church, Newmarket Road in 1839 the parish of Barnwell was served by the Abbey Church – it had been provided in the thirteenth century by the canons of the nearby Barnwell Priory. According to an entry in the National Pipe Organ Register, which, however, gives no source, an organ by Lincoln (*c.*1819) was removed from Christ Church to 'Cavenshaw' in Berkshire and then, in 1879, to Haughton in Staffordshire. If this is correct it seems likely that the organ stood in the Abbey Church rather than Christ Church because the Hill organ (see above) was installed in time for the consecration of the new church in June 1839.

Andrew Freeman, 'Organ cases of the Gothic Renaissance', in *The Organ*, vol. 18 (1939): 144–5

C. H. Davidson, *Sir John Sutton: A Study in True Principles* (Oxford, 1992): 95–8

NPOR: NO4982

ST ANDREW'S STREET BAPTIST CHURCH — St Andrew's Street

The organ was built by Norman & Beard Ltd in 1892 and 1903. It was rebuilt by Ralph Arnold of Orpington in 1971.

GREAT	
Double Diapason	16
Open Diapason I	8
Open Diapason II	8
Clarabella	8
Principal	4
Twelfth	$2\frac{2}{3}$
Fifteenth	2
Mixture (19.22.26)	III
Trumpet	8

POSITIVE	
Gedackt	8
Open Flute	4
Nazard	$2\frac{2}{3}$
Block Flute	2
Tierce (to g^2)	$1\frac{3}{5}$
Larigot (to g^2)	$1\frac{1}{3}$
Trumpet (from Great)	8

COUPLERS
Great to Pedal
Swell to Pedal
Positive to Pedal
Swell to Great 8′
Swell to Great 4′
Swell to Positive
Swell Octave

SWELL	
Open Diapason	8
Stopped Diapason	8
Salicional	8
Voix Celeste	8
Octave	4
Fifteenth	2
Mixture (15.19.22)	III
Contra Fagotto	16
Cornopean	8
Clarion	4

PEDAL	
Open Diapason (wood)	16
Bourdon	16
Principal (from O. Diap. I)	8
Bass Flute	8
Fifteenth (from O. Diap. I)	4
Fagotto (from Swell)	16
Trumpet (from Great)	8

COMPASS
Manuals: C–g^3
Pedal: C–f^1

ACTION
Electric

ACCESSORIES
Four thumb pistons each to Great and Swell (double touch)
Three thumb pistons to Positive
Four toe pistons each to Pedal/Swell and Pedal/Great (double touch)
Reversible toe pistons: Great to Pedal, Swell to Great 8′

The organ was supplied by Hill & Son in 1874, and is said to have been built originally (for another church) by Elliot; it seems to have stood in the north aisle, but was moved by Hill in 1898 to the newly-built organ chamber north of the chancel. Some tonal alterations were made at this time. In 1958 Hill, Norman & Beard rebuilt the instrument, introducing a new console and action, and in 1978 E. J. Johnson & Son redesigned the tonal scheme, adding several new stops.

GREAT

Open Diapason	8
Stopped Diapason	8
Dulciana	8
Principal	4
Fifteenth	2
Mixture	III
Trompette	8

PEDAL

Bourdon	16
Bass Flute (from Bourdon)	8
Choral Bass (from Bourdon)	4
Fagotto	16

ACTION

Electro-pneumatic

SWELL

Stopped Diapason	8
Vox Angelica	8
Flute	4
Principal	2
Oboe	8

COUPLERS

Swell to Great
Great to Pedal
Swell to Pedal
Swell Octave
Swell Octave to Great

COMPASS

Manuals: C–c^4
Pedal: C–g^1

ACCESSORIES

Three thumb pistons each to Great and Swell
Three toe pistons each to Great and Swell

Previous organs

In March 1827 the Vestry resolved that it was 'expedient' that an organ should be acquired for the church and agreed that if £100 could be raised by subscription the remaining cost would be met out of parish funds. The following month they purchased a secondhand organ (eight years old) from the London organ-builder, John Gray; it had a single manual, including two stops in a swell, and was housed in a mahogany case of Gothic design. The final cost was £150. Hill estimated for a new organ in 1855, but it seems that when the west gallery was dismantled in 1865, Gray's instrument was superseded by a harmonium.

CCRO: St Bene't's, Cambridge – Vestry Minutes (1805–49); correspondence relating to installation of organ, 1827; Minutes of Restoration Committee, *c.*1865
BOA: Hill, Norman & Beard Archive – Hill Letter Book (1838–61)

Right:
St Bene't's Church – a nineteenth-century engraving showing the interior looking west, and Gray's organ of 1827.

The organ was described in 1888 as having been recently rebuilt by Nicholson & Co. of Worcester. It then had tracker action. Miller revoiced the organ in 1902, and carried out a reconstruction in 1922, when the action was converted to tubular-pneumatic and further tonal alterations were made.

GREAT		SWELL	
Open Diapason	8	Double Diapason	16
Open Diapason	8	Violin Diapason	8
Claribella	8	Gamba	8
Dulciana	8	Lieblich Gedact	8
Principal	4	Voix Celeste	8
Wald Flute	4	Gemshorn	4
Fifteenth	2	Cornopean	8
Mixture	II	Oboe	8

PEDAL
Bourdon 16
Principal 8

COMPASS
Manuals: C–g^3
Pedal: C–f^1

COUPLERS
Great to Pedals [*sic*]
Swell to Pedals [*sic*]
Swell to Great
Swell Super [*sic*]

ACTION
Tubular-pneumatic

ACCESSORIES
Three thumb pistons to each manual
Three toe pistons to each manual
Two [*sic*] reversible thumb pistons: Great to Pedal
One reversible toe piston: Great to Pedal

Previous organs

An organ was supplied in 1833 by Joseph Warren of Cambridge. This was placed in a west gallery built for the purpose, the organ itself being made by Vincent. It had six stops, a few pedals to draw down the lowest manual keys, and a case painted to resemble wainscot or mahogany. This was presumably the instrument Miller dismantled in 1871 and stored until the restoration of the church was completed. Miller re-erected the organ in the new organ chamber in 1873.

CCRO: St Botolph, Cambridge – Vouchers 1832–3, 1872–5; Warren's estimate 1833; Accounts for organ and gallery (1833–5); proposed case design 1873; Miller's estimate 1902.
Musical Opinion, Vol. XII (1888): 68.

Right:
A sketch (c.1873) of an organ case for St Botolph's. It is not known who drew it but the design was sent to the Revd F. H. Sutton, presumably for his comments. It was never executed

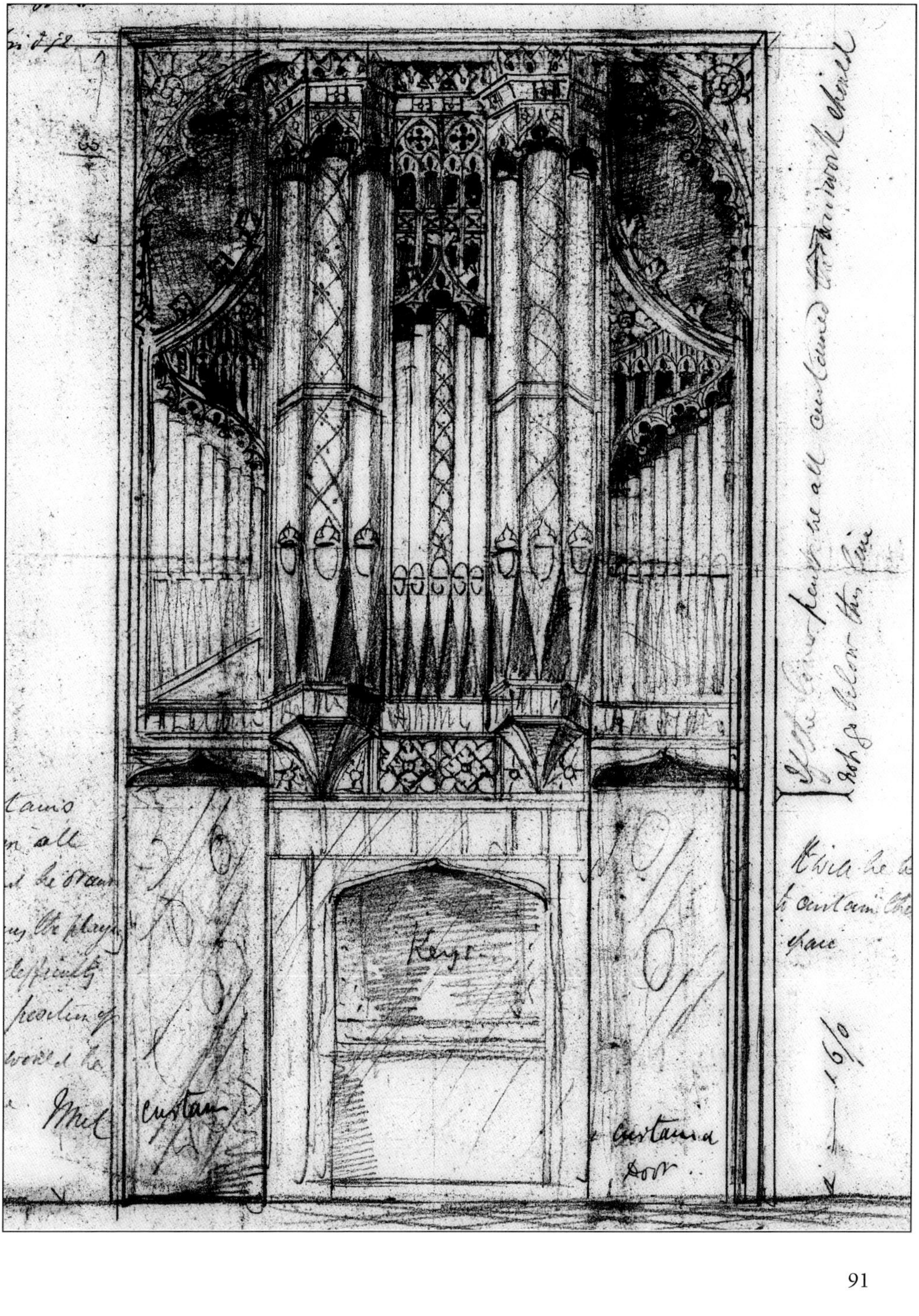
Keys
Curtain
Curtain Door
16/0

ST CATHARINE'S COLLEGE CHAPEL — Trumpington Street

The instrument was built by E. J. Johnson & Son in 1978–80 retaining Thomas Garner's double case of 1894. Much of the Great and all the Swell pipework came from an organ which had stood in the Unitarian Chapel, Little Portland Street, London (from 1862) and subsequently in St James' Church, Watford Fields. The original builders may have been Bishop, Starr & Richardson. The specification of the present organ was drawn up by Dr Peter le Huray, Fellow and Organist of the college. In 2002, Flentrop Orgelbouw (Zaandam) overhauled the organ; the work included the revoicing of the reeds and the provision of new console accessories.

GREAT	
Open Diapason	8
Stopped Diapason	8
Principal	4
Open Flute	4
Nazard	2²/3
Fifteenth	2
Nachthorn	2
Tierce	1³/5
Mixture	II
Scharf	II
Trumpet	8

SWELL	
Stopped Diapason	8
Salicional	8
Voix Celeste	8
Principal	4
Fifteenth	2
Mixture	II–III
Fagot	16
Trumpet	8
Krummhorn	8
Clarion	4
Tremulant	

CHOIR	
Gedeckt	8
Principal	4
Coppel Flute	4
Nasat	2²/3
Octave	2
Spitz Flute	2
Terz	1³/5
Quint	1¹/3
Cymbel	III
Tremulant	

PEDAL	
Principal	16
Dulciana	16
Octave	8
Stopped Flute	8
Fifteenth	4
Nason Flute	4
Mixture	III
Bombarde	16

COUPLERS

Choir to Great
Swell to Great
Great to Pedal
Swell to Pedal
Choir to Pedal
Great & Pedal combinations coupled
Swell & Pedal combinations coupled
Choir & Pedal combinations coupled

COMPASS

Manuals: C–a^3
Pedal: C–f^1

ACTION

Tracker to keys and pedals
Electro-pneumatic to stops

Right:
St Catharine's College Chapel,
organ case by Thomas Garner, 1894.

LAVDATE DOMINVM

ACCESSORIES
Six thumb pistons to each manual
Reversible thumb pistons: Great to Pedal, Swell to Great, Choir to Great
Six toe pistons to Pedal
Reversible toe pistons: Great to Pedal, Swell to Great, Choir to Great
Six general pistons (120 levels)
Six sequencer thumb pistons
One sequencer toe piston
One 'tutti' toe piston
General cancel toe piston

Previous organs

Hill & Son built an organ for the chapel in 1863. It had two manuals and twelve stops, including a short-compass Swell permanently coupled to the Great Stopped Diapason in the bottom octave. Like other Hill organs of the same period, the ivory faces of the stop knobs were stained in different colours to indicate the different departments. It is said that (part of?) this instrument went to Coton Church in 1894.

The following year, a new organ by Norman & Beard was opened. It had three manuals and tubular-pneumatic action. There were plans at this time to extend the chapel, and provision was made to enlarge the organ with Solo and Echo departments, respectively of eight and six stops. It seems likely that the scale of the fine architectural case by Thomas Garner was also influenced by the possible enlargement of the building. In the event, nothing was done, and in 1936 Harrison & Harrison rebuilt the organ, installing a new action and console, and making extensive revisions to the tonal scheme. Later (1962) Compton modified the upperwork of the Great and Choir.

When the new organ was built in 1978–80, the old organ was removed by E. J. Johnson & Son and rebuilt in St John's Church, Upper St Leonard's.

Malcolm Hallowes, 'Some Cambridge college organs', in *Musical Opinion*, vol. 44 (May 1921): 695
Ernest E. Adcock, 'Some organs in Cambridge', in *The Organ*, vol. 32 (1952): 67–8

ST CLEMENT'S CHURCH — Bridge Street

The organ was built by Bryceson Bros. of Brook Street, Euston Road, London as a chancel organ. It dates from the 1860s. Tonal modifications were made during the early years of the twentieth century, when various string-toned registers were introduced. Further changes took place in 1964.

MANUAL	
Open Diapason	8
Stopped Bass (12)	8
Lieblich Gedact (c)	8
Gamba (c)	8
Aeoline (c)	8
Echo Dulciana/Celeste (c)	8
Principal	4
Gross Tierce	$3^1/5$
Viola	2

PEDAL	
Bourdon	16

COUPLER
Manual to Pedal

COMPASS
Manual: C–g^3
Pedal: C–c^1

ACTION
Tracker

Previous organs

According to the *Ely Diocesan Remembrancer*, an organ by Buckwell, rebuilt by Miller, and formerly in St Clement's, Cambridge was installed in Witchford Church in 1896 (information kindly supplied by José Hopkins).

ST COLUMBA'S UNITED REFORMED CHURCH Downing Street

The organ was built by Lewis & Co. in 1891 for the new church. It has since been extensively remodelled by Henry Willis & Sons Ltd (1934), R. H. Walker Ltd (1957), and J. W. Walker & Sons Ltd (1980).

GREAT

Open Diapason	8
Lieblich Gedact	8
Principal	4
Flageolet	2
Sesquialtera	II

SWELL

Geigen	8
Rohr Flöte	8
Aeoline	8
Viola	4
Mixture (15.19.22)	III
Trumpet	8
Tremulant	

PEDAL

Resultant Bass (derived)	32
Bourdon	16
Flute (from Bourdon)	8
Flute (from Bourdon)	4

COUPLERS

Great to Pedal
Swell to Pedal
Swell to Great

ACCESSORIES

Two combination pedals each to Great and Swell

COMPASS

Manuals: C–g^3
Pedal: C–f^1

ACTION

Tracker to keyboards and stops
Tubular-pneumatic to pedals

ST EDWARD'S CHURCH — St Edward's Passage

The organ was built in 1899 by Bedwell & Sons of Cambridge and stood in the North Chapel. In 1964 Hill, Norman & Beard entirely rebuilt Bedwell's instrument. The pipework was re-sited in a chamber created out of the adjoining vestry, and a detached stop-key console was placed in a corner of the chapel.

GREAT	
Open Diapason	8
Stopped Diapason	8
Octave	4
Chimney Flute	4
Twelfth	$2^2/_3$
Block Flute	2
Larigot	$1^1/_3$
Mixture	III

SWELL	
Open Diapason	8
Hohl Flute	8
Echo Salicional	8
Voix Celeste	8
Geigen Principal	4
Lieblich Flute	4
Super Octave	2
Sifflöte	1
Mixture	III
Contra Oboe	16
Trumpet	8

PEDAL	
Sub Bass	16
Lieblich Bourdon	16
Principal	8
Bass Flute (from L. Bdn)	8
Fifteenth (from Prin.)	4
Octave Flute (from L. Bdn)	4
Oboe Bass (from Swell)	16

COUPLERS

Swell to Great
Swell to Great 4′
Swell Super Octave
Swell Sub Octave
Swell to Pedal
Swell to Pedal 4′
Great to Pedal
Great & Pedal combinations coupled

COMPASS

Manuals: C–a^3 (keyboards C–c^4)
Pedal: C–g^1

ACCESSORIES

Four thumb pistons to each manual
Reversible thumb pistons: Swell to Great, Great to Pedal, Swell to Pedal
Four toe pistons each to Pedal and Swell
Reversible toe pistons: Swell to Great, Great to Pedal
'Full Organ' toe piston
Crescendo pedal

Electro-pneumatic action

Previous organs

John Gray supplied a barrel & finger organ with six stops in 1838 at a cost of £176. In 1859 the Chaplain asked the Vestry Meeting for permission to sell this instrument, and stated that a new organ would be required costing around £200. There is no record of who supplied the new organ, although in 1875 it was rebuilt by G.M. Holdich who re-arranged it to fit 'the Organ chamber' (presumably the North Chapel) and completed the compass of the Swell to C. It is possible that parts of this instrument were retained by Bedwell in 1899.

CCRO: St Edward's, Cambridge – Correspondence and vouchers 1838; Holdich's invoice 1875

ST GILES' CHURCH — Castle Street

The organ was built by Miller of Cambridge *c.*1875. It was rebuilt by the same firm in 1918, and then by E.J. Johnson & Son in 1965.

GREAT		
Lieblich Bourdon	16	A
Open Diapason	8	
Stopt Diapason	8	
Principal	4	
Twelfth & Fifteenth	II	

CHOIR	
Stopt Diapason	8
Flute	4
Nazard	$2^2/_3$
Fifteenth	2
Tierce	$1^3/_5$

COUPLERS
Swell to Great
Choir to Great
Swell to Choir
Swell to Pedal
Great to Pedal
Choir to Pedal
Swell Octave
Swell Unison off
Swell Sub Octave

SWELL	
Violin Diapason	8
Lieblich Gedacht	8
Salicional	8
Voix Celeste (c)	8
Gemshorn	4
Mixture	II
Contra Bassoon	16
Trumpet	8

PEDAL		
Open Wood	16	B
Bourdon	16	A
Principal	8	B
Bass Flute	8	A
Octave Quint	$5^1/_3$	A
Fifteenth	4	B

COMPASS
Manuals: C–a^3
Pedal: C–f^1

ACTION
Electro-pneumatic

ACCESSORIES
Three thumb pistons (P, MF, FF) to each manual division
Reversible thumb pistons in each key slip: Swell to Great, Great to Pedal
Three thumb pistons (P, MF, FF) to Pedal in each key slip

Extended ranks are indicated by A and B above.

The organ was built by N. P. Mander Ltd in 1994. The cases by J. Oldrid Scott were retained; they were slightly raised and the lower section of each case was brought forward. A small amount of pipework from the old organ was incorporated in the new scheme (marked*). The consultant was Nicholas Thistlethwaite.

GREAT	
Double Open Diapason	16
Open Diapason I	8
Open Diapason II	8
Stopped Diapason	8
Principal	4
Gemshorn	4
Wald Flute	4
Twelfth	$2^2/_3$
Fifteenth	2
Flageolet	2
Full Mixture (15.19.22)	III
Sharp Mixture (22.26.29)	III
Trumpet	8
Clarion	4
Cornet (c^1)	V

CHOIR	
Open Diapason	8
Gedackt	8
Gamba	8
Principal	4
Flute	4
Nazard	$2^2/_3$
Fifteenth	2
Flautina	2
Tierce	$1^3/_5$
Mixture (19.22)	II
Cremona	8
Tremulant	

SOLO (enclosed, except †)	
Viola da Gamba	8
Viola Celeste	8
Hohl Flute	8
Flauto Traverso	4
Corno di Bassetto	8
Cor Anglais	8
Tremulant	
Tuba	8 †
Trompeta Real (c to c^3) *	8 †

SWELL	
Bourdon *	16
Open Diapason	8
Rohr Gedackt	8
Salicional *	8
Voix Celeste (c) *	8
Principal	4
Stopped Flute	4
Fifteenth	2
Sesquialtera (17.19/12.17)	II
Mixture (19.22.26.29)	IV
Oboe *	8
Vox Humana	8
Double Trumpet	16
Cornopean	8
Clarion	4
Tremulant	

PEDAL	
Subbass *	32
Open Diapason (wood) *	16
Open Diapason (metal)	16
Bourdon (from Subbass)	16
Dulciana *	16
Principal *	8
Bass Flute *	8
Fifteenth *	4
Flute *	4
Mixture (19.22.26.29) *	IV
Contra Trombone	32
Ophicleide *	16
Fagotto *	16
Posaune *	8
Clarion *	4

COMPASS

Manuals: C–a^3

Pedal: C–f^1

Right:
The organ in St John's College Chapel

COUPLERS
Swell to Great
Choir to Great
Solo to Great
Swell to Choir
Solo to Choir
Solo to Swell
Great to Pedal
Swell to Pedal
Choir to Pedal
Solo to Pedal
Solo Octave to Pedal
Great and Pedal combinations coupled
Generals on Swell composition pedals
Full Organ

ACCESSORIES
Eight pistons to each manual (8 levels)
Eight general pistons (64 levels)
Eight composition pedals to Pedal Organ (8 levels)
Eight composition pedals to Swell
Reversible pistons: Choir to Pedal, Great to Pedal, Swell to Pedal, Solo to Pedal, Choir to Great, Swell to Great, Solo to Great, Swell to Choir, Solo to Swell
Reversible pedals: Great to Pedal, Swell to Great, Full Organ
General cancel piston
Cimbelstern

ACTION
Tracker, with parallel electric action to the stops and combination actions
Electric action is used for the Trompeta Real

Previous organs

The college was founded in 1511 on the site of the Hospital of St John the Evangelist. The existing chapel was retained and a list of benefactors drawn up in 1528 records that 'Sondry and divers marchauntes in London gave emongist theyme x^{li} towards the byeing of the newest organs'. A 'lecterne' was provided for the 'orgaines in the quere' in 1557–8, but soon after this Puritanism established a grip on the college, and it is likely that the organs disappeared early in Elizabeth's reign.

With the King's appointment of William Beale as Master in 1634 the character of the college chapel was transformed. In the following year (1635) Robert Dallam 'of the Citty of Westminster Organ-maker' agreed to make a new organ 'to conteyne six seuerall stoppes of pipes euery stoppe conteyning fortynine pipes [viz.] one diapason most part to stand in sight one Principall of Tynne one Recorder of Wood one small Principall of Tynne one two and twentieth of Tynne'. (The missing sixth stop was probably a Stopped Diapason.) It was to cost £185 and was to be completed by July 1636. The construction of a loft cost an additional £30. Dallam returned to repair the organ in 1639 (£2 6s 8d), and in 1640 Henry Jennings received thirty shillings for tuning.

The chapel was a source of scandal to the Puritans who noted that 'at ye west end are a paire of organs set up by Dr Beale, in ye wainscot of wch is a hollow place capacious enough for an image just above ye entrance into ye Chappell ... '. The college decided to take no chances, and in 1643 the junior bursar was paid £2 8s 6d 'for taking down the pictures and the organs and whiting the walls'. Jennings received four shillings 'for taking downe the litle organ'. The demolition was completed the following year, with the payment of 6s 8d to 'old Dowsy when the Organ case was taken away'.

Little is known for certain about the chapel organ after the Restoration. Payments to an organ blower resumed in 1661, and 'Mr Lusemere' [possibly George Loosemore, of Trinity College] received quarterly payments 'for learneing ye Organist'. 'Mr Thaymer' was paid for tuning the organ in 1663, and the accounts record a number of small payments for cord or bellows repairs around this time. Either Dallam's organ had been reinstated or a new instrument provided – the most likely benefactor being Bishop Gunning, who restored the chapel during his mastership (1661–70) and left money at his death to increase the choir's endowment. John Ivory was paid £2 in 1669 'for painting ye case of ye Great Organ, and grounding ye pipes wt blew, & guilding ye Armes & balls at ye top' whilst Thamer received £4 for three weeks work 'mending both ye organs'. There seems to have been an organ in the Lodge at this time – Thamer was paid five shillings for repairing it in 1680, and there are other references in 1685, 1697, 1705 and 1709 – but the entries for 1669 are probably evidence that the chapel organ now had two keyboards. Was the Great case Dallam's? The reference to it being 'taken away' in 1643 possibly implies an attempt at preservation, but later drawings reveal strong affinities with other Cambridge cases of the late-seventeenth century. The question must remain open.

Thamer received regular payments for tuning until 1684. Others were occasionally paid for minor work – Henry Smart (1683, 1686), Edward Smith (1684, 1685) and William Oliver (1686). In 1690, a hammer, tweezers and a pair of pincers were purchased 'for ye Organ'.

Renatus Harris was employed to tune the organ for £5 per annum from 1699. In 1710 he was paid £150 'for worke abt ye Organ vizt. for a new open Diapason, and a new Stop't Diapason, & Additions [to?] ye Basses of principall one Hundred pounds, And for a Trumpet stop and Sesquialter of four Ranks fifty pounds ...' A further £8 11s 11d was expended on commons for his 'servant'. This looks like a reconstruction of the Great Organ, but other details are lacking.

Between 1712 and 1717 several payments were made to Charles Quarles. Then in 1724 Henry Turner spent six weeks repairing the organ, for which he received £30. The Turners tuned the organ until 1776, Barnard Turner also becoming college organist in 1729.

The accounts provide no evidence for major work before the final quarter of the eighteenth century. However, drawings of the organ pre-1838 show an elegant choir case appearing to date (on stylistic grounds) from the second quarter of the century. The only entry that might have any bearing on this is a payment in 1731–2 of £2 5s 0d to 'Smith for five weeks work about ye Organ'. Was 'Smith' a college workman? Or might this have been a gratuity to an organ-builder (Gerard Smith, junior?) whose work had been paid for by a benefactor?

A drawing by H. T. Lilley of the organ in the west gallery of the old St John's College Chapel, as it would have appeared before Hill's work of 1838–9.

Humphrey Argent repaired and cleaned the organ in 1777–8. He tuned it to concert pitch and had his bill made up to £80 'in consideration of the unexpected trouble he has had with it'. John Lincoln was paid for repairs in 1795–6 (£63) and 1806–7 (£29), otherwise maintenance remained in the hands of Argent and his successor, Ling (from 1829).

In September 1838 the college commissioned a new instrument from William Hill at a cost of £690. It was designed by the college organist, Thomas Attwood Walmisley, and stood inside the existing cases, the Great case being extended at the sides to accommodate it. The stop list was a curious hybrid. It retained the old-fashioned long compasses (keys and pedals began at FF), but included such novelties as a French horn, harmonica, claribella and German flute. There were pedal pipes of 24′ pitch and a large Swell division.

Hill's organ had twenty-seven stops and three keyboards. It may have been designed with a view to removal to a new chapel. By the time this was built (1869) the technology and tonal design of organs had moved on, and Hill & Son built what was virtually a new organ costing £1191. It had three manuals and a complete Pedal division, and stood in Scott's elevated chamber on the north side of the chapel. The old cases were disposed of (the Great

Above: Old Bilton Church, Great organ case formerly in St John's College Chapel.
Right: Brownsover Church (near Rugby), chair case from the same instrument.

case to Old Bilton and the Chair case to Brownsover, both near Rugby) but it was not until 1889 that the new organ acquired case fronts, designed by J. Oldrid Scott. Hill & Son made minor alterations at the same time, including the conversion of the pedal and stop actions to pneumatic operation, and the provision of pneumatic levers to Great and Swell.

By the early 1900s when Cyril Rootham was appointed organist the organ was noisy and choked with dirt. Norman & Beard installed tubular-pneumatic action throughout, revoiced the pipework, and made some additions (1902).

Twenty years later (1922) Harrison & Harrison rebuilt the console, installed new drawstop, combination and pedal actions, and carried out an extensive overhaul with some tonal re-balancing.

Hill, Norman & Beard's reconstruction of the organ in 1955–6 had the twin objectives of modernising the action and re-designing the choruses along more classical lines. The old pneumatic actions were electrified and the new console included a generous provision of couplers and other accessories. A fourth keyboard was added (Solo) from which the famous Trompeta Real (projecting, en chamade, from the case) was played. The Choir was re-cast as a 'Positive' division with mutations and a Zimbel, whilst the upperwork of the Great and Pedal was re-modelled. By modifying existing pipework, reducing wind pressures and introducing new registers the builders created a versatile instrument which soon became well-known through recordings and broadcasts as the reputation of the chapel choir under its director, George Guest, grew.

The organ was cleaned and overhauled in 1974. At the same time the composition of the mixtures was reviewed, the Pedal acquired 32′ and 4′ reeds, and a cymbelstern was added.

St John's College Archives: Lease Book (1627–68); Audit Books (1634–1882); Conclusion Book (1736–86)

BL: Harleian MS 7019, f.74

CGA, 6 March 1839

BOA: Hill, Norman & Beard Archives – Hill Letter Book (1838–61), Estimate Book 2 (1862–77)

W&C, vol. 2: 293–5

C.B. Rootham, 'The Chapel Organ', in *The Eagle*, vol. 24 (1902): 77ff

W.L. Sumner, 'The Organs of St John's College, Cambridge', in *The Organ*, vol. 36 (1956): 28–35

Ian Payne, *The provision and practice of sacred music at Cambridge … 1547–1646* (New York & London, 1993): 106

Nicholas Thistlethwaite, 'The new Mander organ in St John's College, Cambridge', in *Organist's Review*, vol. 80 (1994): 7–10

O&A: 37–8, 39–42

ST LUKE'S CHURCH — Victoria Road

The organ was bought from the Parish of St Mary, Whitechapel, London and installed by Hill & Son in 1877. The cost was £250. Lewis cleaned and overhauled the organ in 1917, and the pedal action was pneumaticised by Miller in 1929. During the 1980s, the church nave was converted into a community centre. The chancel was retained as a place of worship for both Anglican and United Reformed congregations. E. J. Johnson & Son reconstructed the organ, making a new building frame and Swell soundboard, re-designing the key and stop actions, and adding a new Pedal Organ. The work was completed in 1993.

GREAT		SWELL	
Open Diapason	8	Double Diapason (c)	16
Stopt Diapason	8	Open Diapason	8
Octave	4	Stopt Diapason	8
Open Flute	4	Octave	4
Octave Quint	$2^2/3$	Super Octave	2
Super Octave	2	Mixture *	II
Sesquialtra (17.19.22)	III	Horn	8
Trumpet	8	Oboe	8

CHOIR		PEDAL	
Stopt Diapason	8	Open Wood	16
Dulciana	8	Bourdon *	16
Octave	4	Principal *	8
Flute	4	Trombone *	16
Fifteenth *	2		

* new stops (1993)

COUPLERS
Swell to Great
Swell to Choir
Great to Pedal
Swell to Pedal
Choir to Pedal

ACCESSORIES
Three composition pedals to Great
Three composition pedals to Swell
Balanced swell pedal

COMPASS
Manuals: C–f^3
Pedal: C–f^1

ACTION
Tracker

History

The Whitechapel organ was opened on 29 May 1715. According to a later source it was built by Christopher Shrider ('Father' Smith's son-in-law and successor). England & Russell added a short-compass six-stop Swell *c.*1780 and Dobson introduced Pedal Pipes and a Dulciana in 1817/1820. In 1855 William Hill undertook an extensive reconstruction of the organ, including new soundboards, a new console, and the modernisation of the pedal arrangements; at the same time, the Swell was extended to tenor c and all the reeds were replaced. Further alterations were made when the organ was removed to Cambridge: four of the Swell registers were completed to C on a separate chest, and a new case ('of stained deal such as they make to most instruments of the present day') was provided.

The organ retains a good deal of eighteenth-century pipework.

RCM MS 1161 ('Organographia')
BOA: Hill, Norman & Beard Archive – Hill Letter Book (1838–61)
C.W. Pearce, *Notes on English organs* (London, 1912): 121

The Hill & Son console (1870) of the organ in St Mary the Great (The University Church).

ST MARY THE GREAT (The University Church) King's Parade

The organ was built originally by 'Father' Smith in 1698. N. P. Mander Ltd renovated the instrument in 1995 and made modest changes to the tonal scheme. A new Pedal chest replaced the electric chests introduced in 1964, the Swell reed chorus was completed, and the console was restored. The organ-builders worked in consultation with Stephen Cleobury (University Organist) and Nicholas Thistlethwaite (consultant).

GREAT		
Bourdon	16	M
Open Diapason	8	Sm
Stopped Diapason	8	Sm
Gamba	8	H
Principal	4	Sm
Nason Flute	4	Sm
Twelfth	$2^{2}/_{3}$	Sm
Fifteenth	2	Sm
Mixture	III	Sm
Trumpet	8	H
Cornet (c^{1})	IV	M
CHOIR		
Stopped Diapason	8	Sm
Dulciana	8	Av
Principal	4	Sm
Flute	4	Sm
Fifteenth	2	Sm
Cremona	8	HNB

COUPLERS
Swell to Great
Swell to Choir
Swell to Pedal
Great to Pedal
Choir to Pedal

COMPASS
Manuals: C–g^{3}
Pedal: C–f^{1}

ACTION
Tracker

SWELL		
Open Diapason	8	T
Stopped Diapason	8	P
Principal	4	T
Fifteenth	2	M
Mixture	III	H
Double Trumpet	16	Av/H
Cornopean	8	M
Oboe	8	H
Clarion	4	Av
PEDAL		
Open Diapason	16	H
Bourdon	16	H
Principal	8	H
Bass Flute	8	H
Fifteenth	4	M
Mixture	II	M
Trombone	16	H

ACCESSORIES
Three composition pedals to Great
Two composition pedals to Swell
Ratchet Swell lever

KEY
pipework wholly or partly by:
Sm = Smith (1698)
T = Turner (1713)
P = Parker (1767)
Av = Avery (1806)
H = Hill (1870)
HNB = Hill, Norman & Beard (1964)
M = Mander (1995)

History

On 18 July 1697 the parish of St Mary the Great consented to a proposal from the Vice Chancellor that an organ should be erected in the church 'at the only cost & charge of the University'. Until the completion of the Senate House in 1730 the church was used as an auditorium for university ceremonies such as the Commencement (the conferment of degrees) as well as for the weekly

University Sermon. Before 1697 the university accounts record payments for organs being brought into the church for special occasions – presumably the authorities then decided that it would be more fitting to have a permanent instrument available in the building.

No contract for either the organ or its wooden gallery has survived, but 'Grumbald' (probably Robert Grumbold, one of a family of Cambridge builders) was paid for 'drawing the scheme of the organ loft' and Bernard Smith received a total of £367 for the organ. The gallery stood at the west end of the nave and was completed by the end of April 1698. Smith and his two 'servantts' arrived at the beginning of May. A Cambridge carrier, Matthew Lancaster, brought parts of the new organ in cases from London and a local carpenter (also called Smith) lent a hand, making 'ye back case of ye bellows', 'a Step for ye Organists foot', and doing various other small jobs. It seems that the organ was substantially complete by the middle of September 1698 when William Carter was paid for 'ye diall-plate & placeing in ye front of ye Organ in St. Mary's' – this refers to the clock face which appeared above the central pipe flat until 1766.

The first thirty years of the organ's existence are marked by frequent expenditure on repairs. An 'Organ Mender' was summoned from London in 1703-4 and paid £60, perhaps to make good damage caused by the Great Storm of November 1703 when it was recorded (with some exaggeration, surely) that a fall of masonry 'battered in pieces a curious Organ lately set up' in the University Church. The 'Organ Mender' was probably Smith himself, for upon his death in 1708 the University paid £80 to his widow 'for repairing the University Organ'. Other work was carried out by Charles Quarles, and then in 1713 Henry Turner added a four-stop 'Eccho' at a charge of £40. In 1721 Christopher Shrider was paid £10 for cleaning and repairing the organ. His bill includes the organ's stop list, enabling the specification at this date to be reconstructed:

GREAT		CHAIR	
(GG, AA, C, D, E–c^3)		(as Great)	
Open Diapason	8	Stop Diapason	8
Stop Diapason	8	Principal	4
Principal	4	Nason	4
Flute	4	Fifteenth	2
Twelfth	$2^2/3$		
Fifteenth	2	ECHO	
Sesquialtera	III ?	(c^1–c^3)	
Trumpet	8	Open Diapason	8
Cornet	IV ?	Principal	4
		Cornet	III ?
		Trumpet	8

The next major work was undertaken by Thomas Parker in 1766–7. Smith's action was replaced, compasses were extended, the pitch lowered and the front pipes regilded. A Vox Humana was added to the Chair Organ, and a Stopped Diapason and a Cremona to the Swell. Parker was paid a total of £267 10s 0d.

John Avery's work in 1804–6 is undocumented. He received £325 – enough to pay for a new wind system, new reeds, a dulciana and an octave of unison

A drawing by H. T. Lilley of the organ in the west gallery of St Mary the Great, as it would have appeared after Hill's reconstruction of 1870.

pedal pipes. Some years later (1819) the gallery was demolished and Thomas Elliot removed the organ to a new stone loft within the tower where it still stands.

By the mid-1860s the University Organist reported the organ to be 'in a state of such complete decay and dilapidation that it cannot be effectively employed to lead and support a choir and congregation in Divine Service'. Following a protracted debate, in which dons argued over the relative merits of organs and scientific laboratories, Hill & Son were commissioned to reconstruct the organ, retaining the case and most of the old pipework, but replacing virtually everything else. Compasses were modernised, the Swell and Pedal were greatly expanded, and Hill added typical Victorian registers to the Great (Bourdon, Cone Gamba) and Choir (Clarinet). The work was completed in 1870.

Little was done to the instrument in the course of the next ninety years. By the 1950s it was in a poor state and discussions began about its future. Various schemes were mooted but the course finally adopted was a conservative one. Certain tonal additions were made in order to reinforce the classical character of the instrument: for example, the Choir gained a Cymbal, Pedal upperwork was introduced on electric action, and the Great acquired a Mounted Cornet and a Spitzprincipal 16′ (adapted from the Cone Gamba). However, the existing pipework was restored sympathetically, and the mechanical actions were retained. The only serious loss was the front pipes. They were reckoned to be beyond repair, but their metal was salvaged to make replacements of the same dimensions. The new pipes were burnished, and gilding was applied to the pipe shades and mouldings of the case, which was stripped down and re-stained under the direction of the church architect, George Pace.

The work was undertaken by Hill, Norman & Beard and completed in 1964.

The Parish Organ

The organ stands to the south of the chancel, above the vestry. It was built by Kenneth Jones and Associates of Bray, Co. Wicklow, and opened by Simon Preston in October 1991.

GREAT	
Double Diapason	16
Open Diapason	8
Rohrflute	8
Octave	4
Spitzflute	4
Superoctave	2
Mixture	II–III
Cimbel	II
Trumpet	8
Tremulant	

SOLO	
Double Diapason	16
Open Flute	8
Wide Octave	4
Nazard	$2^2/_3$
Doublette	2
Wald Flute	2
Tierce	$1^3/_5$
Trumpet	8

COMPASS
Manuals: C–a^3
Pedal: C–f^1

ACTION
Tracker to keys and pedals
Mechanical stop action with parallel electric action for combination system

SWELL	
Salicional	8
Voix Celestes	8
Stopped Diapason	8
Principal	4
Nason Flute	4
Fifteenth	2
Larigot	$1^1/_3$
Sesquialtera	II
Mixture	II–IV
Double Trumpet	16
Cornopean	8
Oboe	8
Tremulant	

PEDAL	
Open Wood	16
Subbass	16
Principal	8
Trombone	16

COUPLERS
Swell to Great
Solo to Great
Great to Pedal
Swell to Pedal
Solo to Pedal
Solo Octave to Pedal

ACCESSORIES
Six pistons to each manual
Eight general pistons
Reversible pistons: Swell to Great, Solo to Great, Great to Pedal, Swell to Pedal, Solo to Pedal
General cancel piston
Setter button
Six combination pedals to Pedal
Eight combination pedals (generals)
Reversible pedals: Swell to Great, Solo to Great, Great to Pedal, Swell to Pedal, and Solo to Pedal (2)
Balanced Swell pedal
Wind control

Previous organs

The churchwardens' accounts for the first half of the sixteenth century contain frequent references to the repair of organs and the payment of organists. An inventory of 1504 records the presence of 'a paier of organs in ecclia'. In 1512–13 the wardens 'payed a blak ffryer in Ester holidais for to play atte Orgayns', and subsequent accounts record expenditure upon locks, leather, and bellows handles, and 3d for 'a quartt of Suett wyne to the orgyn makyr ffor ysse laber' (1527–8). Thomas Canam's payment of eleven shillings for forty-four pounds of tin 'comyng of the olde orgayne pipes' (1542–3) may indicate a new organ or work on an existing one. The organ(s) seems to have been maintained in working order at least until 1564 and inventories of 1568 and 1577 reveal that it was still in existence. However, the inventory of 1583 tells its own melancholy story when it records 'an Orgaine Case with some pypes', and in 1613–14 'mr pawle Tompson' gave the wardens £1 for 'the oargen case'.

The parish was granted the use of the University Organ when the latter was built and proceeded to appoint and pay its own organist. By the late 1860s the organist was having to resort to an harmonium because of the poor state of the Smith organ. Frustrated by the University's procrastination in getting the instrument repaired, the parish decided to install its own organ in the chancel. It was purchased in 1869 at a cost of £400.

The new organ was probably supplied by A. T. Miller. Certainly the Miller firm was responsible for an extensive rebuilding in 1892, which included the application (under licence) of Hope-Jones's patent electric action, and left the organ with three manuals and 35 stops. Miller made various alterations over the years and then in 1961 E.J. Johnson & Son rebuilt the organ with a new electro-pneumatic action and some tonal alterations.

CCRO: St Mary the Great – Audit Books (1635–1880)

CUL: University Archives – Audit Books (1660–1881); Guard Books (1690–1830); Grace Books (1688–1870); Vouchers (1685–1830); miscellaneous papers relating to work in 1697–8 and 1866–70

CGA: 10 April 1839 ('Church Organs in Cambridge')

BOA: Hill, Norman & Beard Archive – Hill Estimate Book, vol. 2 (1862–77)

J.E. Foster (ed.), *The Churchwardens' Accounts of St Mary the Great, Cambridge, from 1504 to 1635* (Cambridge, 1905)

Martin Brayne, *The Greatest Storm* (Stroud, 2002): 7. [The author is indebted to Joan Jeffery for this reference.]

Left:
The Parish Organ in St Mary the Great built by Kenneth Jones (1991).

ST MARY THE LESS — Trumpington Street

The new organ was built by Kenneth Tickell & Company Ltd (Northampton) and installed during 2006–7. The existing case by Lawrence Bond (1978) has been retained.

GREAT		SWELL	
Open Diapason	8	Chimney Flute	8
Stopped Diapason	8	Viola	8
Principal	4	Celeste (c)	8
Spitz Flute	4	Principal	4
Fifteenth	2	Nason Flute	4
Cornet (c)	IV	Flageolet	2
Mixture	IV	Sesquialtera	II
Trumpet	8	Mixture	III
Tremulant		Cremona	16
		Oboe	8
PEDAL		*Tremulant*	
Sub Bass	16		
Principal	8	COMPASS	
Posaune	16	Manuals: C–g^3	
Trumpet (from Great)	8	Pedal: C–f^1	

COUPLERS
Swell to Great
Great to Pedal
Swell to Pedal

ACTION
Tracker to keys and pedals
Electric stop action

ACCESSORIES
Six thumb pistons each to Great and Swell
Six general thumb pistons
Reversible thumb pistons: Swell to Great; Great to Pedal; Swell to Pedal
Setter piston
General cancel piston
Four toe pistons to Pedal
Six toe pistons duplicating generals
Reversible toe pistons: Swell to Great; Great to Pedal

Right:
St Mary the Less, new organ by Kenneth Tickell & Co. Ltd (2006–7).

Previous organs

The first organ of which there is a record was built by Flight & Robson. It was probably a barrel organ and seems to have been acquired towards the end of the 1820s. In 1839 it was sold to Castle Camps Church. William Hill installed a small two-manual instrument in its place which was eventually dismantled (together with its gallery) in 1867. As it appeared that the restoration of the church would be protracted, the parish disposed of Hill's organ to Girton Church (1870) and purchased an harmonium. This served until 1883 when an organ by T. C. Lewis with two manuals and fifteen stops was installed in the former Sunday School room above the vestry. Lewis's instrument had been made for the Fisheries Exhibition in London. Willis added a Quartane to the Swell *c.*1950 and a little later the pedal action was pneumaticised. The cramped siting was far from ideal, and in 1978 Bishop & Son installed an organ in a new gallery built over the south choirstalls. (The Lewis organ went to Holland.) The Bishop organ had two manuals and seventeen stops, and incorporated pipework from an organ of the 1840s which had formerly stood in Necton Church, Norfolk.

CCRO: St Mary the Less, Cambridge – Churchwardens' Accounts (1772–1885); Vestry Minutes (1826–1915)

The present organ was built in 1965 by E.J. Johnson & Son. It incorporates parts of the instrument which previously stood in the church, and the case front and some pipework from an organ by Vowles of Bristol. The latter was built in 1901 for the home of Mr Charrington, the brewer, at Frensham in Surrey, but was later moved to Christ Church, Virginia Water. The Great and Choir Organs and most of the Pedal are sited on a platform above the western arm of the church, whilst the remainder of the pipework is in the old organ chamber on the south-east of the nave. There is a detached console.

GREAT		SWELL	
Contra Dulciana	16	Chimney Flute	8
Open Diapason	8	Salicional	8
Principal	4	Celeste	8
Fifteenth	2	Principal	4
		Fifteenth	2
CHOIR (enclosed)		Quint Mixture	II
Stopped Diapason	8	Contra Oboe	16
Rohr Flute	4	Trumpet	8
Nazat	$2^2/3$	*Tremulant*	
Piccolo	2		
Orchestral Oboe	8	COUPLERS	
		Great to Pedal	
PEDAL		Swell to Pedal	
Sub Bass (derived)	32	Choir to Pedal	
Open Wood	16	Swell to Great	
Bourdon	16	Choir to Great	
Echo Bourdon	16	Swell Sub Octave	
Echo Flute (from Bourdon)	8	Swell Super Octave	
Fifteenth	4	Swell Unison Off	
Twentysecond (from 15th)	2	Swell to Choir	

ACCESSORIES
Three thumb pistons each to Great and Swell, two thumb pistons to Choir
Reversible thumb pistons: Great to Pedal, Swell to Great, Swell to Choir
Three toe pistons to Pedal
Reversible toe pistons: Great to Pedal, Swell to Great, Contra Dulciana 16′

COMPASSES	ACTION
Manuals: C–a^3	Electro-pneumatic
Pedal: C–f^1	

Previous organs

The church was consecrated in December 1866. A few months later, it was recorded that an un-named Fellow of Christ's College had donated an organ. This little instrument had four ranks of pipes and an octave-and-a-half of pedals. By the end of 1869, a short-compass second manual had been added. Twenty years later, A.T. Miller enlarged the organ and moved it from a chamber over the vestry to the floor of the church. The organ was repaired again in 1896, and Miller undertook further repairs and some additions in 1911. An electric blower was introduced in 1949.

Leaflet issued at the opening recital on the rebuilt organ, 16 October 1965; further information from José Hopkins.

St Matthew's Church, case fronts and pipe-work from an organ by Vowles, c.1890.

ST MICHAEL'S CHURCH **Trinity Street**

The church was closed some forty years ago and the nave is now a restaurant. The chancel is still used occasionally for worship, but there is no pipe organ in the building.

Previous organs

A small organ stood in the church in the years following the Restoration. It cannot have been very substantial, because the University occasionally paid for it to be removed to Great St Mary's to accompany University ceremonies.

When Buckwell of Hackney built a new organ in 1832 he was allowed to take away 'the Old Organ now standing in the Church'. Whether this was simply a modest barrel organ or the instrument 'said to have been built by a person named Mott for S. Michael's Cambridge' and erected by Lincoln in Halesowen Church in 1838 (an organ with three manuals) is not known. Buckwell's new organ was a two-manual of reasonable proportions, well thought of by contemporaries. It stood in a gallery, and had a deal painted case with gilt pipes.

The gallery was dismantled in 1859 and the organ was re-sited. Hill & Son repaired it in 1880 and extended the compass of the Swell keys down to C, providing a stopped bass. A more extensive rebuilding followed in 1893 at a cost of £275 – it was undertaken by Miller, who placed the organ behind the south choir stalls.

When the church was closed, E. J. Johnson & Son removed the organ to Guilden Morden, where it remains.

CCRO: St Michael, Cambridge – Buckwell's agreement and bill (1832); Vestry Minutes (1853–88); Audit Book

Sperling Note Books [RCO/BL], vol. 3: 48 (Halesowen)

ST PAUL'S CHURCH — Hills Road

Groves & Mitchell built a two-manual organ for the west gallery of this church in 1849, according to Sperling. It was rebuilt by Forster & Andrews in 1871, and then in 1903 by Miller, who moved it to the north side of the chancel. The organ was again rebuilt in 1961 by Leighton Organs, who provided a detached console on the south side of the church.

GREAT	
Lieblich Bourdon	16
Open Diapason	8
Stopped Diapason	8
Gamba	8
Dulciana	8
Principal	4
Wald Flute	4
Twelfth	$2^2/3$
Fifteenth	2
Tromba	8

COUPLERS

Swell to Great
Swell Sub to Great
Swell Octave to Great
Great Pistons to Pedal
Swell Sub Octave
Swell Octave
Swell Unison Off
Solo Tromba on Swell
Swell to Pedal
Swell Octave to Pedal
Great to Pedal

COMPASS

Manuals: C–a^3
Pedal: C–f^1

ACTION

Electro-pneumatic

ACCESSORIES

Four thumb pistons to each manual
Four toe pistons each to Swell and Pedal
Reversible toe piston: Great to Pedal

Sperling Note Books [RCO/BL], vol. 1:35

SWELL	
Open Diapason	8
Stopped Diapason	8
Orchestral Gamba	8
Voix Celeste (c)	8
Principal	4
Nazard	$2^2/3$
Fifteenth	2
Mixture	III
Double Trumpet	16
Trumpet (from D. Trumpet)	8
Oboe	8
Clarion (from D. Trumpet)	4
Tremulant	

PEDAL	
Acoustic Bass (derived)	32
Open Diapason (wood)	16
Bourdon	16
Lieblich Bourdon (Great)	16
Bass Flute (from Bourdon)	8
Double Trumpet (Swell)	16

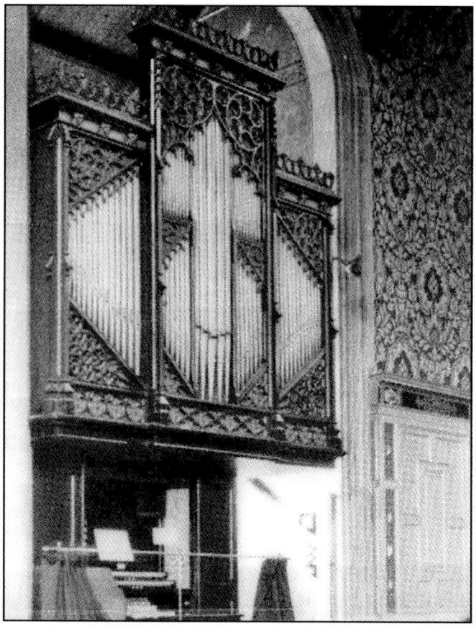

Left:
St Paul's Church, the organ in 1929, with the console below the case-front.

Above:
The organ in St Paul's Church after the 1961 rebuild

A new organ was installed in the chapel in 2004 by Orgues Létourneau of St Hyacinthe, Quebec, Canada, with the following specification.

GRAND-ORGUE	
Bourdon	16
Montre	8
Flûte à cheminée	8
Prestant	4
Flûte conique	4
Doublette	2
Fourniture (19.22.26.29)	IV
Cornet (12.15.17)	III
Trompette	8
Tremblant	

PÉDALE	
Contrebasse	16
Soubasse	16
Violoncelle	8
Basse de chorale	4
Bombarde	16
Trompette	8

RÉCIT EXPRESSIF	
Viole de Gambe	8
Voix céleste (G)	8
Cor de nuit	8
Prestant	4
Flûte octaviante	4
Octavin	2
Plein Jeu (15.19.22.26)	IV
Basson	16
Trompette harmonique	8
Hautbois	8
Tremblant	

POSITIF DE DOS	
Bourdon	8
Prestant	4
Doublette	2
Larigot	$1^1/_3$
Clarinette	8

COUPLERS

Récit au Grand-Orgue
Positif au Grand-Orgue
Récit au Positif
Grand-Orgue à la Pédale
Récit à la Pédale
Positif à la Pédale

COMPASS

Manuals: C–a^3
Pedal: C–g^1

ACTION

Tracker to keys and pedals
Electric to stops

ACCESSORIES

Six thumb pistons to Grand-Orgue
Eight thumb pistons to Récit
Four thumb pistons to Positif
Six thumb and toe pistons to Pédale
Reversible thumb pistons to inter-manual couplers
Reversible thumb and toe pistons to Pédale couplers
Tutti pistons (thumb and toe)
Ten general thumb pistons, duplicated by toe pistons
Setter piston (128 memory levels)
Sequencer

Right:
The new Létourneau organ (2004) in Selwyn College Chapel

Previous organs

The first organ to stand in the west gallery of the chapel had a single manual and pedals, and was supplied by J. W. Walker & Co. in the 1890s. Rushworth & Dreaper enlarged and reconstructed this instrument in 1935, adding a second manual and simple casework. Harrison & Harrison installed a new 21-stop organ with mechanical key action and electric stop action in 1975. This was later sold to St Andrews University and was replaced with an instrument made by E. J. Johnson & Son, incorporating pipework from a Holdich organ of 1845, built originally for Kettering Parish Church. The Johnson organ was completed in 1994 by Peter Collins.

Selwyn College Chapel, the organ by Harrison & Harrison Ltd., installed in 1975, as it appeared in 1983.

SIDNEY SUSSEX COLLEGE CHAPEL — Sidney Street

The organ was built by Harrison & Harrison in 1963. It was enlarged and re-designed by E.J. Johnson & Son (1985) in consultation with Dr Peter le Huray. The college has confirmed (2008) that it intends to commission new instruments by Flentrop Orgelbouw (Holland) and Taylor & Boody (USA).

GREAT		SWELL	
Open Diapason	8	Gedeckt	8
Stopped Diapason	8	Principal	4
Octave	4	Octave	2
Super Octave	2	Tierce	$1^3/5$
Block Flute	2	Larigot	$1^1/3$
Mixture	IV	Mixture	III
Mounted Cornet	IV	Fagotto	16
		Trumpet	8

PEDAL		COUPLERS
Subbass	16	Swell to Great
Principal	8	Great to Pedal
Stopped Flute	8	Swell to Pedal
Octave (from Principal)	4	Swell Octave
Mixture	III	Swell Sub Octave
Bombarde	16	Swell Unison Off
		Great to Pedal Combinations

COMPASS
Manuals: C–c^4
Pedal: C–g^1

ACTION
Electro-pneumatic

ACCESSORIES
Five thumb pistons each to Great and Swell
Five toe pistons to Pedal
One thumb piston: 'Oboe 8ft'
Reversible thumb pistons: Great to Pedal, Swell to Great, and Pedal Bombarde
One reversible toe piston: Great to Pedal

Previous organs

A Casson Positive was installed in the west gallery when the chapel was rebuilt in 1910–12. Some ten years later this was replaced with a secondhand organ of six stops built by Henry Fincham which went (in 1963) to the church at Wickmere.

TRINITY COLLEGE CHAPEL **Trinity Street**

The organ was built by Metzler of Zurich in 1975–6 within the restored main case of 1708 and the earlier Chair case; registers marked with an asterisk in the specification incorporate pipework from the Bernard Smith organ. Metzler overhauled the instrument in 2001.

HAUPTWERK	
Principal *	16
Octave *	8
Hohlflöte	8
Octave *	4
Spitzflöte	4
Quinte *	2²/3
Superoctave *	2
Sesquialter	III
Mixtur	IV–V
Cornett	IV
Trompete	8
Vox Humana	8

PEDAL	
Principal *	16
Subbass	16
Octavbass	8
Bourdon	8
Octave	4
Mixtur	V
Posaune	16
Trompete	8
Trompete	4

COUPLERS
Rückpositiv to Hauptwerk
Schwellwerk to Hauptwerk
Hauptwerk to Pedal (pedal)
Rückpositiv to Pedal (pedal)
Schwellwerk to Pedal (pedal)

ACTION
Tracker to keys and pedals
Mechanical stop action

RÜCKPOSITIV	
Principal *	8
Gedackt	8
Octave	4
Rohrflöte	4
Octave	2
Gemshorn	2
Larigot	1¹/3
Sesquialter	II
Scharf	III
Dulcian	8
Tremulant	

SCHWELLWERK	
Viola	8
Suavial	8
Rohrflöte	8
Principal	4
Gedackt Flöte	4
Nasard	2²/3
Doublette	2
Terz	1³/5
Mixtur	IV
Fagott	16
Trompete	8
Tremulant	

COMPASS
Manuals: C–f^3
Pedal: C–f^1

ACCESSORIES
Two composition pedals to Hauptwerk
One reversible pedal to Posaune
(all mechanical)

Right:
The Metzler organ in Trinity College Chapel, photographed in July 1976 during the inaugural conference of the British Institute of Organ Studies (BIOS).

Previous organs

Trinity College was founded by King Henry VIII in 1546. Its creation was made possible by the suppression of two existing foundations, King's Hall and Michaelhouse, and the chapel of the former was at first used by the new college. An unnamed organ-maker received 16s 8d in 1547/8 'whan he sett up the orgaynes', and 'Tomson' was paid two shillings 'for mendyng the organs at sundry times' in 1549/50. In 1554/5 twelve pence was expended in 'fetchynge the Orgayne mender fro[m] Roysto[n]'; William Manne received sixteen shillings 'for caradge of the organ', and the 'carte mane' was given three pence for his trouble.

The Statutes of 1560 provided for a chapel foundation consisting of four priests, six lay clerks, ten choristers, and an organist and master of the choristers. The new chapel was finished in 1567, but it is not clear if the payment of 8s 6d to 'Thomas [the] singyng man & two others that toke downe ye organs in ye chappell' in 1564/5 refers to the old or the new chapel. Certainly, there is no record of organs being installed in the new chapel, so although the singers and the master of the choristers appear regularly in the accounts over the next thirty years, it is possible that there was no organ, and that the 'instrument' mended by Hugh [Rose?] in 1585/6 was another keyboard instrument or an organ elsewhere in the college.

The fortunes of the chapel music revived (as Ian Payne has shown) following the appointment of Thomas Nevile as Master of Trinity in 1593. In 1594 Hugh Rose was paid £6 13s 4d 'for the Organe', and Andrew Chapman (carpenter) received £24 'for the frame [i.e. case?] of the Orgayne'. A further 47s 2d was spent on 'yron worke belonginge to the Organe', 4s 6d on 'nayles', and £3 'for mr Pooleys organe' (a borrowed intrument?). Rose's work may have taken some time: he received £6 in 1594–5, and a further £5 in 1595-6 'for fynishing the Orgaines'. This sounds like a new organ rather than an old one being brought back into use. Rose was paid 6s 8d for tuning the organ in 1597. A few years later (1603/4) 'the Organ mender' received £3 'for tuninge, makinge the bellowes, and tuninge of the stopps', and a joiner was paid 41s 8d 'for a Perriment [sc. pediment] on the topp of the organs wth the Scrowles and 7 bowles for the same'. The same account records a payment of 2s 8d for a 'henge for the newe doore and a [latch?] wth a crowes foote for the topp of ye Organes'.

A significant addition was made in 1609/10 when £40 was paid to John York 'for makinge the newe chaire orgaine', and £13 5s 6d to Knuckle 'for painting & guilding thereof'. (It is perhaps no coincidence that King's had acquired a two-manual organ a year or two before this.) The existing organ was spruced up at the same time: York was paid £42 'for his owne work and his mans about the mending of the ould organ and for tynn, lead and other newe [materials]', whilst 'Russell ye painter' received £8 10s 'for painting and guilding the ould organ-pypes & the Case therof'. Thirty shillings was expended on 'ironworke for the organes', and eight shillings was paid to the sawyer 'for sawing the Clapbord and making a lather for the use of the organ'.

York received £4 in 1612 for mending the organs; he was assisted by two labourers and a joiner. A further 12s was spent on 'six deales for stopps'. More work was required in 1613–14. 'John' (presumably York) was paid

30s 10d 'for mending of the organs him selfe and his man for twentie dayes and for parchement, leather, glewe, &c'. Later in the year, he received two more payments, each of 13s 4d, and 2s 6d 'for mending the smale organe'; nine shillings was spent on 'leade for the Organ'. About this time John York disappears from the records, perhaps to reappear in Oxford where one 'Yorke' was responsible for maintenance of the organ in Magdalen College between *c*.1616 and 1637. At Trinity he was succeeded by 'Ctopher Brittaine' (possibly related to Stephen Bretton, or Brittaine, a Norwich organ-builder) who was paid no less than £25 in 1614–15 for repair and unspecified new work. Brittaine received £4 for maintenance in 1617/18, and it seems that this was an annual allowance. Sadly, the accounts from 1622–37 are lost, but by 1639/40 the allowance was being paid to 'Mr Dalham'.

Shortly before this, the chapel had been re-ordered along Laudian lines. Over £500 was spent, including £50 for gilding and painting the organs (1636). However, this reform was shortlived. Entries in the accounts for 1642/3 tell a familiar story. In that year, the organ blower was paid his usual stipend (£2) 'for not blowing ye organs', whilst George Woodruffe received 15s 'for taking downe ye organs & hanginge' and 'Mr Jenings' was paid 45s 'for taking downe ye Organ pipes'. The following year (1643/4) the college spent 1s 6d 'for removing Mr Ramseys things' – this was Robert Ramsey, the college organist.

With the Restoration of 1660 the college moved speedily to restore the choral service. During the second quarter of the year, £1 10s was paid 'for removeing, setting upp and tuneing the Little Organ', college workmen were paid small sums for work in the organ loft, and a candlestick was purchased 'to be used at the Organ'. George Loosemore was the organist. He was paid for mending the organs in 1660–1, and then in 1662–3 'for removeing his owne Organ' (was this the 'Little Organ'?). The reason for the removal was the completion of a new organ by Thomas Thamer. He was paid a total of £120 during 1661–3, and his men received £5 'at the finishing the Organ'. Nothing is known about this instrument, except that Thamer regularly received small sums for tuning, mending or cleaning it until his death in 1685. In the following year (1685–6) 'Mr Tho: Smith' was paid £1 6s 'for putting ye Organ into Tune'. Later the same year, Denson (one of the lay clerks) received £10 for 'ye First paymt upon ye Articles betweene him & Mr Smith towards making an Organ'. Curiously, nothing more is heard of this until 1693–4 when the payment of £111 'to Mr Bernard Smith at severall times for ye New Organ (besides 29li. 16s. 6d paid by ye Steward for his mens Commons & sizings)' is recorded. At the same time, small sums were paid for 'Symphony's' (instrumental accompaniments) at the opening of the organ, and for minor works in the organ loft.

These entries mark the beginning of 'Father' Smith's connection with the college, but it is by no means clear what is meant by the 'New Organ'. Did it supersede Thamer's instrument? Or was it an addition to it? It has been suggested that the existing Chair case is earlier in date than the main case of 1708. So did Smith add a Chair Organ to a Great Organ by Thamer? Unfortunately, the college archives cast no further light on the matter.

Smith received £10 in 1694–5 (his final payment?). There are then no references to the organ until 1705, when Charles Quarles, the college organist, was paid £10 'for mending the organ'.

Left:
The west-facing front of the organ in Trinity College Chapel.

Right:
Trinity College Chapel showing the organ case as it appeared before 1913. In 1870 Hill had carried out a complete reconstruction and modernisation of the organ. The east and west fronts of the main case were enlarged by the addition of flats and towers in the same style as the eighteenth-century work.

During the Mastership of Dr Bentley (1700–42) the chapel was repaired and completely refitted. This work (and its cost) was a source of considerable friction between Bentley and the Fellowship, and one of the contentious items was the provision of a new organ. According to Bentley's enemies, he had promised 'the old organist, one of his Club, whom he called Father Smith, that he should make the College an Organ, soon after he was Master'. When Smith took Bentley at his word and went ahead with making the organ, the Master was obliged to initiate a major refurbishment of the chapel to accommodate it. The instrument reputedly cost £1500. How much is true remains unclear, but there is no doubt that Smith was commissioned to make a new organ. It probably had three keyboards (Great, Chair and Echo), was housed in the two surviving cases, and stood on the screen, then seventeen feet east of its present position. When Smith died before the work was completed, the college ordered that Christopher Shrider – Smith's son-in-law – 'do finish the organ by tuning and voicing it; and that he be allowed so much ... as Her Majesties Organists shall think reasonable' (May 1708).

Shrider returned in 1715 when he was paid £30 'for ye swelling stops' (presumably, the conversion of an Echo Organ into a Swell) and a further £30 'for cleaning and voicing ye Chapel Organ'. It remained in his care until 1734.

Barnard Turner succeeded him, and overhauled the organ in 1747. Twenty years later, Thomas Parker, 'Organ Maker in London', was paid £185 for unspecified repairs and improvements (1767). John Avery undertook further work in 1801–2 (£240), John Lincoln in 1808 (£116), and Flight & Robson in 1819. The latter took the college to court for refusing to pay for 'extras' and were awarded £106. Few details have survived of any of these contracts, though one of the later rebuildings must have included provision of a rudimentary pedal board and a few pedal pipes.

The organ was again rebuilt in 1835–6 by John Gray when the compass of the Great was taken down to CC [16'], couplers, composition pedals and German pedals were added, several reed stops were replaced and other tonal changes made in keeping with the taste of the day. Walmisley, the organist, requested the addition of a 'melody coupler' [Choir to Pedal 2'] so that he could solo the tune of the National Anthem in the introduction to Attwood's 'I was glad'. The work cost £410. In 1853 the Great soundboard was replaced

and its tonal scheme modified (£230), and two years later a Violone 16' was introduced to supplement the single Pedal stop – a 32′ Bourdon. This work was done by Hill, who, in 1870, carried out a complete reconstruction and modernisation costing £2,500; the east and west fronts of the main case were enlarged by the addition of flats and towers in the same style as the eighteenth-century work, hydraulic engines were introduced, and the instrument was left with 59 stops and four manuals.

This was the organ over which C. V. Stanford presided during his first years at Trinity (he was appointed organist in 1874). Presumably, he was responsible for changes made in 1876, including a radiating pedal board, the centralising of the Swell pedal, and the enclosure of five Solo registers. In 1889 over £1500 was spent in substituting tubular-pneumatic action for the existing tracker action and providing a new console. A number of tonal alterations were made to the Great and Choir. The Chair case was brought back into use to house a 'Front Choir' of four stops, and the antechapel was disfigured by standing the basses of the 32′ open wood in its NW corner. This work was undertaken by Hill & Son.

In 1913 the organ was rebuilt by Harrison & Harrison. The 74-stop scheme was drawn up nominally by Alan Gray (appointed Stanford's successor in 1893), but it represented a typical Harrison specification of the period, with a massive twenty-stop Great capped by a five-rank Harmonics, and a generous allowance of the usual trombas and orchestral voices. The console was to the standard Harrison design and the action was a mixture of tubular- and electro-pneumatic. Most of the old pipework was comprehensively revoiced. This instrument was dismantled in 1975, and only the surviving cases and pipework by Smith were retained for restoration and re-use in the new Metzler organ.

Trinity College Archives: Senior Bursar's Audit Books (1550–1712); Conclusion Books; John Gray's Estimate, 25 May 1835

BOA: Hill, Norman & Beard Archive – Hill Letter Book (1838–61) and Estimate Book, vol. 2 (1861–77)

W&C, vol. 2: 574–7, 580–1

Alan Gray (ed.), *A brief history of the Organ in the Chapel of Trinity College, Cambridge*, by G. F. Cobb (Cambridge, 1913)

Malcolm Hallowes, 'Some Cambridge college organs', in *Musical Opinion*, vol. 44 (April 1921): 611

Ian Payne, 'The musical establishment at Trinity College, Cambridge, 1546–1644', in *Proceedings of the Cambridge Antiquarian Society*, vol. 74 (1985): 53–69

JWD: 173-5

Jeremy Dibble, 'Stanford and the organ recitals at Trinity College, Cambridge, 1872–1890', in *JBIOS*, vol. 18 (1994): 158–70

O&A: 31–4, 44

José Hopkins, 'Footnotes to Cobb's account of the organ of Trinity College, Cambridge', in *JBIOS*, vol. 29 (2005): 45–51

TRINITY HALL CHAPEL — Trinity Lane

A new organ by Carsten Lund (Denmark) was installed in 2006. The consultant was David Sanger.

GREAT		SWELL	
Bordun	16	Viola da Gamba	8
Principal	8	Flauto traverso	8
Rohrflute	8	Fugara	4
Octave	4	Gedackt	4
Cone flute	4	Gemshorn	2
Quinte	$2^2/_3$	Mixtur	III
Octave	2	Oboe	8
Tierce	$1^3/_5$	*Tremulant*	

PEDAL	
Subbas	16
Bordun (transmission)	16
Principal (transmission)	8
Gedackt (transmission)	8
Fagotto	16

COUPLERS
Swell to Great
Swell 16' to Great
Great to Pedal
Swell to Pedal
Swell 4' to Pedal
Great & Pedal combinations coupled
Swell & Pedal combinations coupled
Generals on Swell toe pistons

COMPASS
Manuals: C–g^3
Pedal: C–f^1

ACCESSORIES
Five thumb pistons to each manual
Five toe pistons to Pedal
Five toe pistons to Swell
General combination system with: 2 x five general pistons, with 8000 combinations divided into eight user ranges
Two thumb pistons (up/down) for level selection
Four step thumb pistons (forward/reverse)
Set, shift and cancel pistons
Two-step toe pistons
Mobile Ventus (wind control)

ACTION
Tracker key action
Tracker and electrical action to stops

Previous organs

In 1981 E.J. Johnson & Son installed a mechanical action organ with two manuals and fifteen stops; it replaced a small instrument by Harrison & Harrison, dating from the inter-war years.

Trinity Hall Chapel, the new organ by Carsten Lund (Denmark) which was installed in 2006.

UNITARIAN CHURCH — Emmanuel Road

The organ was built by Miller & Son in 1928, and given in memory of Sydney and Edith Martineau. It is reputed to be A. H. Miller's last new organ.

GREAT	
Open Diapason	8
Dulciana	8
Clarabella	8
Principal	4
Wald Flute	4

SWELL	
Open Diapason	8
Lieblich [*sic*]	8
Salicional	8
Voix Celeste	8
Principal	4
Oboe	8

PEDAL	
Bourdon	16
Bass Flute	8

COUPLERS
Swell to Great
Great to Pedal
Swell to Pedal

ACCESSORIES
Three composition pedals to Great
Three composition pedals to Swell
Balanced Swell pedal

COMPASS
Manuals: C–a^3
Pedal: C–f^1

ACTION
Tracker to keys and stops
Tubular-pneumatic to pedals

UNIVERSITY MUSIC SCHOOL **West Road**

The eighteenth-century chamber organ now housed in the University Music School was once the property of Captain Oates of Antarctic fame. The case is veneered in mahogany and the front pipes are metal dummies. Noel Mander restored the instrument *c.*1968, but an earlier attribution to John Snetzler must now be considered suspect. Whoever was its original builder, the organ can be confidently dated to the third quarter of the eighteenth century.

LEFT HAND	RIGHT HAND
Sesquialtra Bass [to b]	Principal Treble* [c^1]
Fifteenth	Cornet [c^1]
Flute	Open Diapason [c^1]
Stopt Bass [to b]	Stopt Diapason [c^1]

* this replaced a hautboy enclosed in its own swell when the organ was restored

COMPASS
GG, C, AA, D–e^3

ACTION
Tracker

MIXTURE

GG	17.19.22
g#	15.17.19
c^1	12.15.17

Michael Wilson, *The English Chamber organ,* (Oxford, 1968): 103-4
Alan Barnes and Martin Renshaw, *The life and work of John Snetzler,* (London, 1994): 275

The chamber organ in the University Music School.

WESLEY CHURCH — Christ's Pieces

The organ was installed by F.H. Browne & Sons of Canterbury in 1990. It came from Eastbrook Hall (Methodist Mission), Bradford and was originally the work of William Hill (1845). Hill's organ had 42 stops (including a seven-stop Pedal Organ) and was housed in an imposing Spanish mahogany case. Whilst still in Bradford the instrument was rebuilt by Hill & Son in 1875 and 1904, and again by Marshall Sykes (Leeds) in 1959. On its removal to Cambridge, it was extensively reconstructed and the casework was adapted to suit the new location. Much of the original Hill pipework survives in the Great and Swell Organs.

GREAT

Double Diapason	16
Open Diapason 1	8
Open Diapason 2	8
Stopped Diapason	8
Dulciana	8
Quint	$5^1/3$
Octave	4
Harmonic Flute	4
Tenth	$3^1/5$
Twelfth	$2^2/3$
Fifteenth	2
Sesquialtera	V
Mixture	III
Trumpet	8
Clarion	4

CHOIR

Open Diapason	8
Stopped Diapason	8
Viol di Gamba	8
Gemshorn	4
Flute	4
Nazard	$2^2/3$
Flageolet	2
Tierce	$1^3/5$
Clarinet	8
Tuba *	8
Tuba Clarion *	4
Tremulant	

ACTION

Electro-pneumatic

COUPLERS

Swell to Great
Swell to Choir
Choir to Great

SWELL

Open Diapason	8
Stopped Diapason	8
Echo Gamba	8
Voix Celeste	8
Principal	4
Open Flute	4
Twelfth	$2^2/3$
Super Octave	2
Mixture	III
Contra Fagotto	16
Cornopean	8
Oboe	8
Clarion	4
Tremulant	

PEDAL

Acoustic Bass	32
Open Wood	16
Open Metal	16
Sub Bass	16
Principal (from Open Met.)	8
Bass Flute (from Sub Bass)	8
Twelfth	$5^1/3$
Octave	4
Octave Flute (from Sub Bass)	4
Sesquialtera	V
Trombone *	16
Clarion *	8
Krummhorn	4

* Reeds extended from one rank

ACCESSORIES

Six thumb pistons to each manual division
Five reversible thumb pistons:
Swell to Great, Choir to Great, Great to Pedal, Swell to Pedal, Choir to Pedal

COUPLERS (*continued*)
Swell Octave
Swell Sub Octave
Great to Pedal
Swell to Pedal
Choir to Pedal

COMPASS
Manuals: C–c^4
Pedal: C–g^1

ACCESSORIES (*continued*)
Six thumb pistons (generals)
General cancel
Setter button
Six toe pistons to Swell Organ
Six toe pistons to Pedal Organ
Reversible toe pistons:
Swell to Great, Great to Pedal
Great and Pedal combinations coupled (switch)

Previous organs

An organ said to be by Forster & Andrews was bought secondhand for the old Hobson Street Chapel in 1869. Thirty years later A. T. Miller & Son modified this instrument, and then in 1920 used it as the basis for the organ in the new chapel. It was overhauled by Hill, Norman & Beard in 1959, when a new electro-pneumatic action was fitted and some minor tonal alterations were made. The organ then had three manuals and twenty-five stops.

Nicholas Thistlethwaite, *The making of the Victorian organ* (Cambridge, 1990): passim

Wesley Church, the Hill organ (1845) formerly in Eastbrook Hall, Bradford, divided and re-configured to suit its new location.

ZION BAPTIST CHURCH — East Road

The organ was built by J. Porritt of Leicester in 1887. Minor modifications have been made, including the addition of a balanced swell pedal and the substitution of a mixture for the original clarionette; otherwise, the organ is little altered.

GREAT	
Open Diapason	8
Stop Diapason	8
Gamba	8
Dulciana	8
Principal	4
Wald Flute	4
Fifteenth	2
Mixture	II

SWELL	
Lieblich Bourdon	16
Open Diapason	8
Lieblich Gedakt	8
Vox Angelica	8
Principal	4
Piccolo	2
Cornopean	8
Oboe	8
Tremulant [removed]	

PEDAL	
Open Diapason	16
[Spare slide]	

COUPLERS
Swell to Great
Great to Pedal
Swell to Pedal

ACCESSORIES
Five composition pedals

COMPASS
Manuals: C–g^3
Pedal: C–f^1

ACTION
Tracker

APPENDIX

A selection of interesting organs within one hour's drive of Cambridge.

BOXWORTH

Holdich chamber organ of 1857, formerly in Stirtloe Hall, given to Boxworth in 1953. The keyboard compass commences at GG. There are seven ranks of pipes (four of them with an extra top octave for use with the 'Diaocton' coupler), one octave of pedal pull-downs, and a general swell.

COLNE

Chamber organ by G.P. England (*c.*1810) with five ranks. The keyboard compass was reduced to C–f^3, probably when Miller moved the organ into the new church *c.*1900.

COTON

One manual organ with seven stops, built by E.J. Johnson & Son in 1968. It incorporates parts of the previous organ, which was reputed to include pipework from both Great St Mary's and St Catharine's College. The richly-coloured Gothic case (*c.*1860?) is a cheerful ornament.

DRY DRAYTON

Small three-manual by Brindley & Foster (1881), with characteristic late-Victorian string and flute registers. The action is tracker, and the instrument was restored by Peter Collins Ltd in 1997.

ELY CATHEDRAL

Important tonal scheme by Harrison & Harrison (1907), much modified and enlarged in 1975 and again in 2001. But the case (1851) is still magnificent, the design being based by Sir Gilbert Scott on the famous case (1497) which hangs high above the nave of Strasbourg Minster.

GODMANCHESTER

Large two-manual built by Bryceson & Fincham in 1860, and comparatively little altered since. The thirteen-stop Great Organ boasts two mixtures and two reeds, and both divisions exhibit a selection of the novelty stops beloved of the Victorians. A restoration by Peter Collins Ltd in 1994 included the consolidation of the Pedal Organ, added in 1976. Still a period piece, complete with its original mechanical action and console.

GOODERSTONE (Norfolk)

A fine chamber organ of *c.*1830, no maker's plate, but possibly the work of J. C. Bishop. There are four composition pedals and just seven stops. The handsome case is made of mahogany. Richard Bower restored the instrument in 2001.

GRAVELEY

Ten-stop, one-manual Holdich of *c.*1855, formerly at Papworth St Agnes. The style of the whole is a charming anachronism when one considers the

Left:
The G.P. England chamber organ in Colne Parish Church.

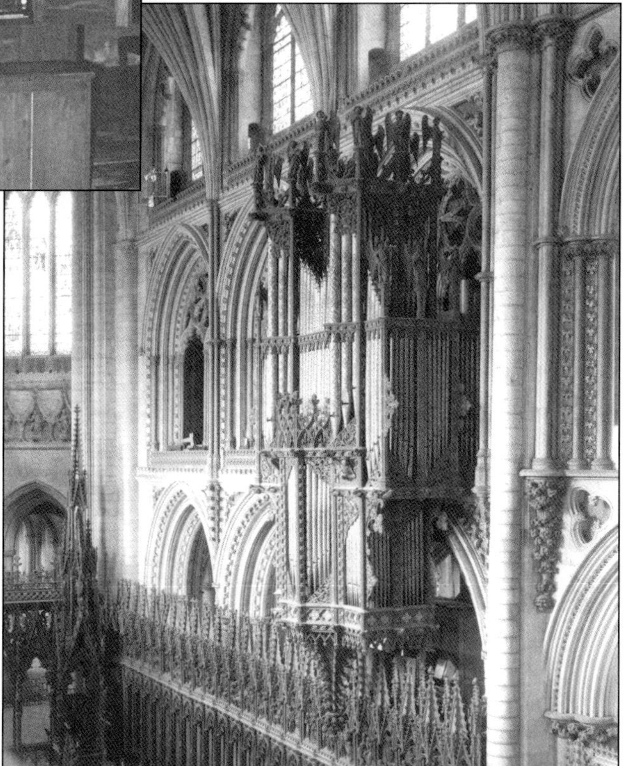

Right:
Ely Cathedral, the organ by Harrison & Harrison Ltd with casework designed by Sir Gilbert Scott, 1851.

Left:
Great Bardfield (Essex),
organ of c.1866.

Right:
Harlton Church,
Bishop & Starr organ of c.1869
before its removal to the west gallery (2008).

developments of the previous decade – case with three flats in a naïve Gothic, black-headed stop knobs with square shanks, and paper labels above.

GREAT BARDFIELD (Essex)

Shallow chancel organ of *c.*1866 with a distinctly ecclesiological feeling. The design and colouring of the case is reminiscent of others conceived under Sutton influence. A very bold, bright chorus. The builder was probably A. T. Miller – he certainly worked here at some stage, as the console testifies.

HARLTON

Delightful, Sutton-influenced case of *c.*1869. The upper part of the case has two flats and a centre tower containing surprisingly effective silvered pipes. The organ (originally built by Bishop & Starr) is being reconstructed by Peter Bumstead in a new west gallery (2008).

HASLINGFIELD

Two manual organ by J.C. Bishop (1847), built originally for Holy Trinity, Paddington. It was moved to Ely Parish Church in 1882 and survived without major alteration until 1977. During the 1990s, the instrument was acquired by Haslingfield Parish Church, and was sympathetically restored by Peter Bumstead; a new Gothic case was provided. The original console survives, and the Great and Swell specifications are largely intact.

MELDRETH

Built originally as a barrel organ by Joseph Walker, who then added a keyboard in 1856. Ten years later it left its first home (Bassingbourn Church) and was sold to Meldreth for £100. Though some original upperwork has disappeared it is worth mentioning on account of the barrel mechanism which still functions. There are three barrels.

ST NEOTS

G.M. Holdich built a substantial three-manual organ in 1855. A rebuilding in 1900 led to the removal of some characteristic Holdich features, but a further reconstruction in 1972 (by Bishop & Son) endeavoured to restore the instrument to something of its original character. Most of Holdich's Great and Swell have survived, and the manual divisions are still on mechanical action.

SOUTH PICKENHAM (Norfolk)

Originally commissioned by Sir John Sutton for West Tofts (1857) where it stood in a swallow's nest gallery over the choirstalls. The exquisite Gothic case has painted doors and was made in Ghent – Pugin seems to have been involved in its design. Bishop built the organ, but the pipework was 'finished' by a Belgian voicer. Miller added pedal pipes and a tiny *Brustwerk* in 1881. The instrument had to be moved to South Pickenham in 1950 following the army's appropriation of the district around West Tofts for training purposes.

TADLOW

A four-stop finger organ by T.C. Bates (*c.*1850?) in a neat Gothic case. It was provided with a 'dumb organist' which survives but is not in working order.

Left:
South Pickenham (Norfolk), organ originally built for West Tofts Church in 1857.

Right:
Thaxted Church (Essex), organ built by Henry Cephas Lincoln in 1821.

THAXTED (Essex)

One of the most important survivals from the period before continental influences brought about a radical change in English organ design. This three-manual instrument with FF-compass Great and Choir, and rudimentary pedal provision, was made by H. C. Lincoln for St John's Chapel, Bedford Row, London in 1821. It was removed to Thaxted later in the century. The case reveals a rich blend of architectural and natural motifs, the whole having a pronounced Regency flavour. Now in regrettably poor condition.

THORNEY ABBEY

The organ incorporates pipework by Flight (1790), Robson (1840) and Bevington (1858). In its present disposition it is the work of Hill & Son (1888). There are eighteen stops spread over two manuals. The splendid Gothic revival case is probably the work of Dr A. G. Hill.

TITCHMARSH (Northamptonshire)

Two manual organ by T. C. Lewis (1870) in original condition. It has thirteen stops and produces a fine stirring sound.

WITCHFORD

A two-manual organ of twelve stops in a Gothick case. The Great appears to represent the original instrument (*c.*1830) to which a Swell was added, perhaps by Bevington, whose label appears inside the cresting around the top of the case. Various traditions associate the organ with Haddenham, Exeter and an unidentified girls school in Cambridge, but the *Ely Diocesan Remembrancer* suggests that it was built by Buckwell, rebuilt by Miller, and then moved to Witchford from St Clement's, Cambridge, in 1896. Johnson restored the organ in 1974.

INDEX OF PEOPLE AND PLACES

Organ-builders' names are set in Bold.

SELECT BIBLIOGRAPHY

Primary source material relating to the history of many of the organs recorded in this volume is to be found in college archive collections and in the surviving records of particular churches. Most of the latter are now deposited in the Cambridgeshire County Record Office.

Other important (though not always reliable) MS sources should be mentioned: the Sperling Note Books, formerly in the Royal College of Organists and now in the British Library (BL Music Loan 79), together with various nineteenth-century collections of specifications (such as Leffler's note book, partially transcribed by C. W. Pearce *c.*1900 as *Notes on English Organs*), and the business records of organ-building firms. The most substantial collection of the latter is held in the British Organ Archive (under the auspices of the British Institute of Organ Studies, and currently housed in the archives department of Birmingham Central Library); the extant records of the firms of Hill & Son, and Norman & Beard Ltd are preserved there and have proved invaluable in tracing the history of certain Cambridge organs.

Among a great deal of printed material, attention should be drawn to occasional articles in *The Organ* (London, 1921–) and the *Journal of the British Institute of Organ Studies* (Oxford, 1977–), and to the following:

'Church Organs in Cambridge', nos. 1–3, in *The Cambridge General Advertiser*, 1839 (6 March, 10 April, 22 May).

Cecil Clutton and Austin Niland, *The British Organ*, London, 1963 (i) and 1982 (ii).

C. H. Davidson, *Sir John Sutton – A study in true principles*, Oxford, 1992.

The Revd W. E. Dickson, 'Old Times in Cambridge', in *Musical Opinion*, April 1893: 398.

The dictionary of organs and organists, London, 1921 (ii).

Andrew Freeman, *Father Smith*, London, 1926. Reissued, with additions by John Rowntree, Oxford, 1977.

Malcolm Hallowes, 'Some Cambridge college organs', in *Musical Opinion*, vol. 44 (April–June 1921): 611–12, 695, 775.

Frida Knight, *Cambridge music*, Cambridge, 1980.

Ian Payne, *The provision and practice of sacred music at Cambridge colleges and selected cathedrals, 1547–1646*, New York and London 1993.

The Royal Commission on Historical Monuments, *The City of Cambridge*, London, 1959.

John Rowntree and John Brennan, *The classical organ in Britain*, (3 vols), Oxford, 1975, 1979 and 1993.

T. A. Walmisley, 'Organs', in *Cambridge Portfolio* (ed. John James Smith), Cambridge, *c.*1838.

Robert Willis and John Willis Clark, *The architectural history of the University of Cambridge*, (3 vols) Cambridge, 1886.

ACKNOWLEDGEMENTS AND SOURCES OF ILLUSTRATIONS

The author would like to extend his thanks to all those who have made information available to him or loaned photographs for use in this book, among them

The British Library, The British Organ Archive, Cambridgeshire County Record Office, Cambridge University Library, Christ's College Library (Professor G.T. Martin), Emmanuel College Library, Jesus College Archives (Dr Frances Willmoth), King's College Library (Dr Rosalind Moad), Peterhouse Library (Dr Roger Lovatt), Trinity College Library (Jonathan Smith), The National Monuments Record, and The Royal College of Organists.

John Bailey (Bishop & Son), Ian Bell, Dr Paul Binski, Timothy Brown, John Budgen, Timothy Byram-Wigfield, Stephen Cleobury, Philip Coad, Peter Collins (Peter Collins Ltd), T.B. Corfield, Canon Hilary Davidson, Dr Martin Ennis, Kelland Everitt, Alexander Ffinch, Frank Fowler, Dr Gerald Gifford, †Michael Gillingham, A.J. Gosden, Dominic Gwynn (Goetze & Gwynn), †Dr George Guest, Charles Hall (Norman Hall & Sons Ltd), †E. Holt, Daniel Hyde, Eric Impey, Carl Jackson, Joan Jeffery, William Johnson, Kenneth Jones (Kenneth Jones & Associates), Hans Gerd Klais (Johannes Klais Orgelbau), †Dr Peter le Huray, Sarah MacDonald, John Mander (Mander Organs), Dr Richard Marlow, Dr William McVicker, Peter Meadows (University Archivist), E. Norman, A.E.B. Owen, Anne Page, D.O.M. Parsons, Dr Ian Payne, Robert Pennells (J.W. Walker & Sons Ltd), Nicholas Plumley, F. Roney, Dr David Rowland, David Sanger, Christopher Saward, Richard Sharp, R.A. Starkey, Graham Sudbury, Paul Tindall, Mark Venning (Harrison & Harrison Ltd), Dr Geoffrey Webber, †Donald Wort, and Joan Wrycroft.

Photographers and sources of illustrations:

Geoffrey Batty, Cambridge: 140
R. von Beckerath (E. Leigh, Cambridge): 26
John F. Brennan, Oxford: 19, 22, 28, 34, 35, 41, 46, 49, 67, 68, 79, 84, 86, 89, 93, 108, 110, 114, 120, 123, 129, 138, 147
Cambridge Records Office (Revd D. Walser): 91
Peter Collins Ltd: 39
B.B. Edmonds Collection: 16, 17, 27, 53, 64, 84, 104, 105, 122, 144
Andrew Freeman Collection: 31, 47, 59, 72, 85
Kate Grillet Photography: 43
Harrison & Harrison Ltd. (Ramsey & Musprat, Cambridge): 126
King's College, Cambridge: 61, 62
Edward Leigh, Cambridge: 101
Carston Lund, Denmark: 136
N.P. Mander Ltd: 30, 71, 75
National Monuments Record, London: 133
Orgelbau Kuhn AG, CH–Männedorf ©: 51
Orgues Létourneau, Quebec: 125
Positif Press, Oxford: 15, 21, 112, 132, 143, 146
Royal College of Organists: 34, 72
Nicholas Thistlethwaite: 143
Kenneth Tickell & Company Ltd: 117